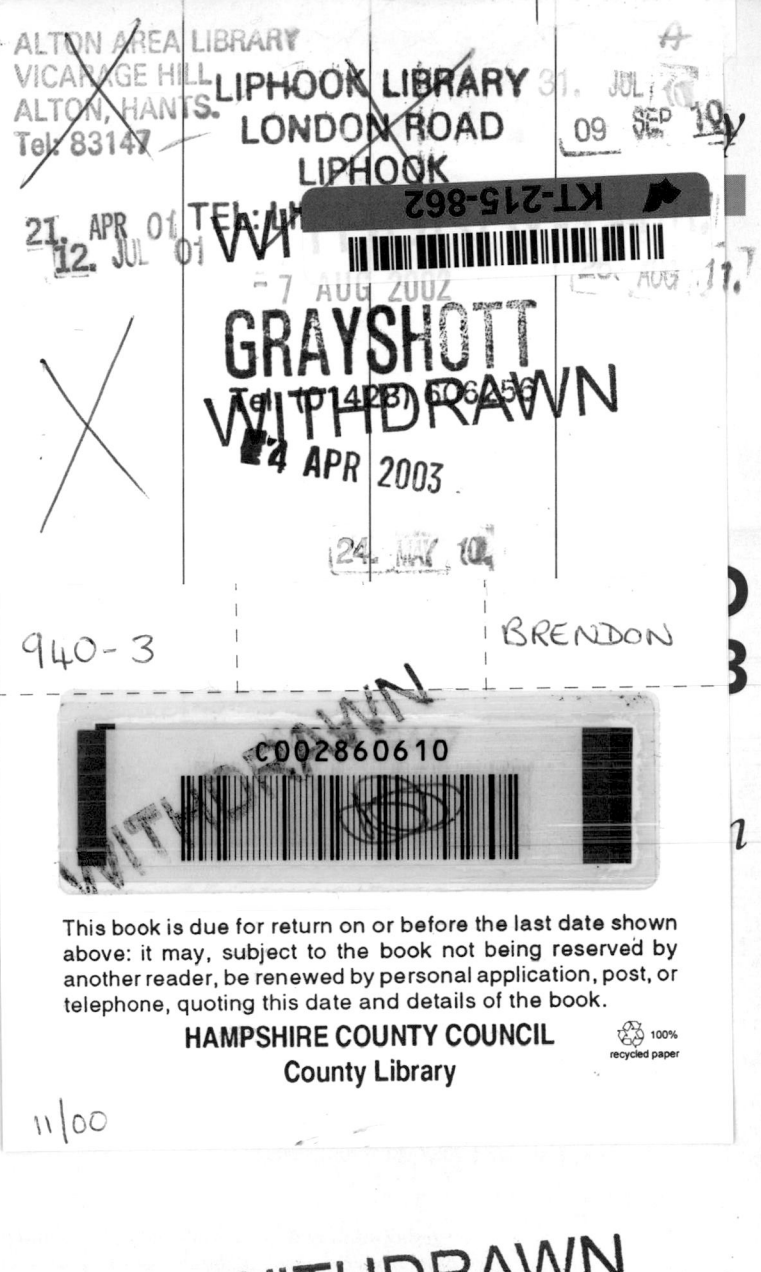

Hodder & Stoughton

A MEMBER OF THE HODDER HEADLINE GROUP

Orders: please contact Bookpoint Ltd, 78 Milton Park, Abingdon, Oxon OX14 4TD.
Telephone: (44) 01235 827720, Fax: (44) 01235 400454. Lines are open from
9.00–6.00, Monday to Saturday, with a 24 hour message answering service. Email
address: orders@bookpoint.co.uk

British Library Cataloguing in Publication Data
A catalogue record for this title is available from The British Library

ISBN 0 340 74303 4

First published 2000
Impression number 10 9 8 7 6 5 4 3 2 1
Year   2005 2004 2003 2002 2001 2000

Typeset by Fakenham Photosetting Ltd, Fakenham, Norfolk.
Printed in Great Britain for Hodder & Stoughton Educational, a division of Hodder
Headline Plc, 338 Euston Road, London NW1 3BH by Redwood Books, Trowbridge,
Wilts.

Acknowledgements

I should like to thank Dr Jay Winter of Pembroke College, Cambridge and Mary Brown of St Mary's School, Cambridge for their advice and help. I am also grateful to the staff of the Departments of Documents and Art at the Imperial War Museum, who gave me valuable assistance in delving into their rich archive of First World War material.

The cover illustration shows the painting 'Leuchtkugel', G 1917/13 by Otto Dix © DACS 2000

The publishers would like to thank the following for permission to reproduce copyright material in this volume:
Abacus for extracts from *Letters From a Lost Generation* by A Bishop and M Bostridge (Eds.) (1999); A M Heath & Co. Ltd. for the extract from *Three Soldiers* (Copyright © J Dos Passos, 1990), and the extract from *Dark Continent* (Copyright © Mark Mazower, Allen Lane, 1998); A P Watt Ltd. on behalf of Sir Martin Gilbert CBE for an extract from *The First World War* by M Gilbert; Arnold Publishers for extracts from *The First World War: Germany and Austria-Hungary 1914–1918* by H Herwig, (1997) and for the extract from *Gallipoli Diary* by I Hamilton (1920); Berg Publishers for the extract from *Men at War* by Audoin-Rouzeau (1992); Blandford Press for the extract from *The Sailor's War* by P Liddle (1985); The Bodley Head for extracts from *A War Imagined* by S Haynes (1990); Cambridge University Press for the extract from 'Women and Work in Wartime Britain' by D Thom in *The Upheaval of War* by R Wall and J Winter (1988); Constable & Robinson Publishing Ltd. for the extract from *A Nurse at the Russian Front* by F Farmbrough (1974), and from *True First World War Stories* by Jon E Lewis (Ed.) (1997); Jonathan Cape for extracts from *People's Tragedy* by Orlando Figes (1996); Chatto & Windus for the extract from 'Strange Meeting' from *The Poems of Wilfred Owen*, (edited by E Blunden, 1955); Victor Gollancz for the extract from *Testament of Youth* by Vera Brittain (1993); Faber and Faber Ltd. for extracts from *Diaries 1915–1918 by Siegfried Sassoon* (Ed.), R Hart-Davis (1983); P G Heath for an extract from *Forty Years After* by P G Heath (unpublished manuscript held at by the Imperial War Museum, London); The Historical Association for extracts from 'The Peace Settlement' by Z Steiner and 'The Entry of the USA into War and its Effects' by D Trask from *First World War* by H Strachan; Hutchinson for extracts from *The First World War* by J Keegan (1998); W Keylor, *The Legacy of the Great War* Copyright © 1998, by Houghton Mifflin Company; S Marks, 'The Myths of Reparations' in *The Legacy of the Great War* by W Keylor Copyright © 1998 by Houghton Mifflin Company; The First World War Archives Department, Imperial War Museum for extracts from *Outline: an Autobiography and other Writings* by Paul Nash; Macmillan Publishers Ltd. for extracts from *1918: Year of Victory* by M Brown (1998), *The Imperial War Museum Book of the First World War* by M Brown (1991), *Imperial War Museum of the Western Front* by M Brown (1993), *Europe: The Last Hundred Years* by A C Morales (1979), *Defeat at Gallipoli* by N Steel and P Hart (1994), *At the Heart of a Tiger* by G Dallas (1993) and *The Deluge: British Society and the First World War* by A Marwick (1991); Pearson Educational Limited for extracts from *Modern Italy 1871–1982* by M Clark, *Origins of the First World War* by J Joll (1984) and *The Decline of the Liberal Party* by P Adelman (1995); Pen and Sword Books for extracts from *Veterans* by R Van Emden and S Humphries (Leo Cooper, 1998), 'Austria-Hungary' by M Cornwell in *At The Eleventh Hour* by H Cecil and P Liddle (Leo Cooper, 1998), 'The American Soldier in France' by J Cooke, 'Italy and the War in the Adriatic' by R Sicurezza, 'The Russian Soldier's Morale from the Evidence of Tsarist Military Censorship' by I Davidian and 'Ernest Junger: Storm Trooper and Chronicler' by T Nevin all from *Facing Armageddon* by H Cecil and P Liddle (Leo Cooper, 1996); Oxford University Press for an extract from *Origins of the War of 1914* by L Albertini (translated by I Massey, 1957); Penguin UK for extracts from *1914–1918 Voices & Images of the Great War* by Lyn MacDonald, (1988), *First World War Prose* by J Glover and J Silkin (1989), *The Complete Saki* by Saki (1982), *The Great War* by J Winter and B Baggett (1966); *Akenfield: Portrait of an English Village* by R Blythe (Allen Lane, 1969), *Hitler, 1889–1936* by Ian Kershaw (Allen Lane, 1998) and *The Pity of War* by Niall Ferguson (Allen Lane, 1998); Siegfried Sassoon for an extract from *The Complete Memoirs of George Sherston* by Siegfried Sassoon (copyright © Siegfried Sassoon by kind permission of George Sassoon); Spellmount Publishers for extracts from *The Irish Guards in the Great War: The Second Battalion* by Rudyard Kipling (1997).

The publishers would also like to thank the following for permission to reproduce copyright illustrations:
Bystander Newspaper, London Evening News, page 43; Hulton Getty, page 64; Imperial War Museum, pages 31, 32, 83, 105, 139, 140; Robert Opic Collection, page 141.

Every effort has been made to trace and acknowledge ownership of copyright. The publishers will be glad to make suitable arrangements with any copyright holders with whom it has not been possible to contact.

Preface

The original *Access to History* series was conceived as a collection of sets of books covering popular chronological periods in British history, together with the histories of other countries, such as France, Germany, Russia and the USA. This arrangement complemented the way in which history has traditionally been taught in sixth forms, colleges and universities. In recent years, however, other ways of dividing up the past have become increasingly popular. In particular, there has been a greater emphasis on studying relatively brief periods in considerable detail and on comparing similar historical phenomena in different countries. These developments have generated a demand for appropriate learning materials, and, in response, two new 'strands' have been added to the main series – *In Depth* and *Themes*. The new volumes build directly on the features that have made *Access to History* so popular.

To the general reader

Access books have been specifically designed to meet the needs of examination students, but they also have much to offer the general reader. The authors are committed to the belief that good history must not only be accurate, up-to-date and scholarly, but also clearly and attractively written. The main body of the text (excluding the Study Guide sections) should therefore form a readable and engaging survey of a topic. Moreover, each author has aimed not merely to provide as clear an explanation as possible of what happened in the past but also to stimulate readers and to challenge them into thinking for themselves about the past and its significance. Thus, although no prior knowledge is expected from the reader, he or she is treated as an intelligent and thinking person throughout. The author tends to share ideas and explore possibilities, instead of delivering so-called 'historical truths' from on high.

To the student reader

It is intended that *Access* books should be used by students studying history at a higher level. Its volumes are all designed to be working texts, which should be reasonably clear on a first reading but which will benefit from re-reading and close study.

To be an effective and successful student, you need to budget your time wisely. Hence you should think carefully about how important the material in a particular book is for you. If you simply need to acquire a general grasp of a topic, the following approach will probably be effective:

1. Read Chapter 1, which should give you an overview of the whole book, and think about its contents.
2. Skim through Chapter 2, paying particular attention to the 'Points to Consider' box and to the 'Key Issue' highlighted at the start of each section. Decide if you need to read the whole chapter.
3. If you do, read the chapter, stopping at the end of every sub-division of the text to make notes.
4. Repeat stage 2 (and stage 3 where appropriate) for the other chapters.

If, however, your course demands a detailed knowledge of the contents of the book, you will need to be correspondingly more thorough. There is no perfect way of studying, and it is particularly worthwhile experimenting with different styles of note-making to find the one that best suits you. Nevertheless the following plan of action is worth trying:

1. Read a whole chapter quickly, preferably at one sitting. Avoid the temptation – which may be very great – to make notes at this stage.
2. Study the diagram at the end of the chapter, ensuring that you understand the general 'shape' of what you have read.
3. Re-read the chapter more slowly, this time taking notes. You may well be amazed at how much more intelligible and straightforward the material seems on a second reading – and your notes will be correspondingly more useful to you when you have to write an essay or revise for an exam. In the long run, reading a chapter twice can, in fact, often save time. Be sure to make your notes in a clear, orderly fashion, and spread them out so that, if necessary, you can later add extra information.
4. The Study Guide sections will be particularly valuable for those taking AS level, A level and Higher. Read the advice on essay questions, and do tackle the specimen titles. (Remember that if learning is to be effective, it must be active. No one – alas – has yet devised any substitute for real effort. It is up to you to make up your own mind on the key issues in any topic.)
5. Attempt the source-based questions. The guidance on tackling these exercises is well worth reading and thinking about.

When you have finished the main chapters, go through the 'Further Reading' section. Remember that no single book can ever do more than introduce a topic, and it is to be hoped that, time permitting, you will want to read more widely. If *Access* books help you to discover just how diverse and fascinating the human past can be, the series will have succeeded in its aim – and you will experience that enthusiasm for the subject which, along with efficient learning, is the hallmark of the best students.

Robert Pearce

1 The Causes of the War

POINTS TO CONSIDER

As you read this chapter try to make up your own mind about who or what should be blamed for the outbreak of war. Was Germany more to blame than other countries? Were military leaders, politicians or ordinary people most responsible for causing this catastrophic conflict?

KEY DATES

1871	Creation of German Empire after victory over France	
1882	Triple Alliance between Germany, Austria and Italy	
1894	Dual Alliance between France and Russia	
1898	Beginning of German naval building programme	
1902	Alliance between Britain and Japan	
1904	Entente between Britain and France	
	War between Russia and Japan leading to Japanese victory	
1905	Tangier crisis	
1907	Triple Entente between Britain, France and Russia	
1908	Austrian annexation of Bosnia	
1911	Agadir crisis	
	Secret naval agreement between Britain and France	
	Italian annexation of Libya	
1912	First Balkan War	
1913	Second Balkan War	
1914	28 June	Assassination of Archduke Ferdinand of Austria
	5 July	German assurance of support to Austria
	23 July	Austrian ultimatum to Serbia
	28 July	Austrian declaration of war on Serbia
	30 July	Full mobilisation of Russian troops
	1 August	German declaration of war on Russia
	3 August	German declaration of war on France
		German invasion of Belgium
	4 August	British declaration of war on Germany
	6 August	Austrian declaration of war on Russia

1 Introduction

> If any question why we died,
> Tell them, because our fathers lied.[1]

Britain's imperialist poet Rudyard Kipling wrote these lines as one of his *Epitaphs of the War* in 1919, four years after the death of his only son John on the Western Front. Simple though the words seem, they can be interpreted in several ways. Kipling himself had actually told less than the truth to get his 17-year-old son made an army officer in spite of his short sight. He had also painted an extravagant picture of 'the Hun menace' in speeches urging many other young men to enlist. But it is unlikely that Kipling's grief caused him to reject his previous convictions. The poem was probably intended to accuse pre-war Liberal statesmen of misleading the British public about the true danger of a European conflict. Whatever Kipling meant, his lines raise the poignant question of who or what caused the deaths of John and over eight million other servicemen (of all nationalities) between 1914 and 1918.

2 Debating the War

> **KEY ISSUE** Why has there been so much controversy over the causes of the First World War?

Because the war was so devastating, participants, politicians and historians have argued fiercely about its causes. In the same year as Kipling wrote his *Epitaphs*, the Treaty of Versailles explicitly placed the guilt for 'all the loss and damage' of the war on the defeated Germans and their allies. This clause was bitterly denied by Germany in post-war years and soon became a subject of keen debate among historians of all countries. In the 1920s and 1930s the idea of a more general responsibility gained ground in both political and academic circles. Blame was placed on general factors such as secret diplomacy, economic rivalry, the arms race or imperialism. Hence it was thought that every country shared the guilt. Britain's war Prime Minister, David Lloyd George, summed up this view when he wrote in his *War Memoirs* that 'the nations in 1914 slithered over the brink into the boiling cauldron of war without any trace of apprehension or dismay'.[2]

The Second World War, however, prompted a reassessment of Germany's responsibility for the First. In his vast book the Italian journalist Luigi Albertini concluded that the 'full and final responsibility for the outbreak of war' should be laid on premature German mobilisation – though he noted that other countries 'showed no great fear of the tempest that was being unloosed'.[3] The German historian Fritz Fischer angered his compatriots in 1961 when he blamed the war on Imperial Germany's 'grab for world power status' and drew parallels with Nazi policies.[4] These works have led to much re-examination of the evidence and continuing debate. Some historians accept Fischer's interpretation, others seek to modify it, while still others draw attention to the general 'war mentality' of Europe in 1914. The rest of this chapter is devoted to this contentious issue, starting with the sequence of events which led immediately to the conflict.

3 Going to War

> **KEY ISSUE** Why did the Great Powers go to war with each other in August 1914?

The war broke out six weeks after the assassination, on 28 June 1914, of Archduke Franz Ferdinand, heir to the throne of the Austro-Hungarian Empire. He was killed while on an official visit to Sarajevo, the capital of Bosnia, as a protest against the inclusion of this Slav province in the vast Habsburg empire. The young student who shot the Archduke was a Bosnian Serb, a member of a Slav nationalist organisation based in neighbouring Serbia. Although the Austrian Emperor Franz-Joseph was not much upset by the death of his nephew and his 'low-born' wife Sophia, he made it clear that this slight to Austrian honour could not go unpunished.

Before taking any action against Serbia he sought the backing of Austria's ally Germany. On 5 July Kaiser William II of Germany promised 'full support' even if this should mean war with Russia, the traditional protector of the Slavs; indeed he encouraged the Austrians to 'make use of the present moment'.[5] On 23 July the Austrian government sent Serbia an ultimatum described by Britain's Foreign Secretary, Sir Edward Grey, as 'the most formidable document I had ever seen addressed by one State to another that was independent'.[6] It demanded that Serbia suppress all anti-Austrian 'subversion' and accept the assistance of imperial officials in carrying this out. Within the 48-hour limit the Serbian government sent a conciliatory reply agreeing to most of the demands but questioning the right of Austria to interfere in its internal affairs. Determined to deal with the Serb 'menace', the Emperor rejected this reply and on 28 July declared war and immediately began to bombard Belgrade, the capital of Serbia.

In the meantime the French President Poincaré and Prime Minister Viviani had been on a long-planned visit to St Petersburg, where they had cordial but indecisive discussions with their Russian allies. Diplomatically isolated during their boat cruise home, the French leaders played no part in European events between 25 and 29 July. By the time they arrived in Paris, the French Commander-in-Chief, General Joffre, had taken matters into his own hands by promising the Russian military attaché 'full and active support'.

Over the next few days events moved fast with decisions increasingly being taken by soldiers. On 29 July the Russian army was partially mobilised so that it would be ready to aid Serbia by attacking the north-east frontier of the Austrian Empire. The next day Tsar

Nicholas II was persuaded by his ministers and generals to declare full mobilisation, allowing Russian troops to advance also towards Germany's eastern border. Now that Russia had made the first move, German Chancellor Bethmann Hollweg could announce mobilisation without seeming to have acted aggressively. Urged on by his military chiefs, the Kaiser declared war on Russia on 1 August. When Poincaré refused to withdraw support for Russia, Germany also declared war on France (3 August). Privately Poincaré expressed his relief that the blame for a war which France had not sought could clearly be placed on Germany: 'Never before had a declaration of war been welcomed with such satisfaction'.[7]

Britain, despite much diplomatic pressure, had so far given no commitment to France or to Russia, the two countries with which it had signed ententes (friendly agreements). After failing in several attempts at mediation, Grey had tried to persuade the cabinet that Britain would face a 'miserable and ignoble future' if it did not join in a conflict which could result in German domination of the Continent and the high seas. But he was not sure of political or popular backing until 3 August when German troops prepared to invade Belgium in accordance with General Schlieffen's plan for the conquest of France (see page 10). Thus Britain, pledged since 1839 to uphold Belgium's independence, declared war on Germany on 4 August.

Austria-Hungary, preoccupied with its Serbian campaign, did not formally declare war on Russia until 6 August. But it seems clear, as recent historians assert, that the outbreak of general war was put in train by the empire's determination to settle accounts with Serbia. 'For too long,' writes Holger Helwig, 'Anglo-Saxons refused to accept that the home of *SacherTorte* and *Kaffee mit Schlag* [cake and coffee with cream] could have initiated the great folly of 1914.'[8]

All the other participants claimed at the time to be embarking on war for defensive reasons. Tsar Nicholas II's justification on 2 August was that his country had 'to intercede not only for a related country [Serbia], unjustly attacked, but also to safeguard the honour, dignity, and integrity of Russia, and her position among the Great Powers'. The Kaiser stated on 4 August: 'The present situation is the result of an ill will which has been active for many years against the power and prosperity of the German Empire. In a defensive war which has been forced upon us, with a clear conscience and a clean hand, we take up the sword.' On the same day President Poincaré asserted that German incursions across the French eastern frontier on 1 August meant that France had become 'the object of a brutal and premeditated aggression which is an insolent defiance of international law'. And H.H. Asquith, Britain's Prime Minister, argued on 6 August that Britain was 'fighting to vindicate the principle that small nationalities are not to be crushed, in defiance of international good faith, by the arbitrary will of a strong and overmastering power'.[9]

Were these protestations of injured virtue genuine or were they special pleading (or indeed lies) designed to gain popular support for war? The question of guilt or innocence can only be determined by an examination of the background to the events of July–August 1914.

4 Explaining the War

> **KEY ISSUE** Which source of long-term international tension was most responsible for the outbreak of world war?

a) The Alliance System

Many countries went to war because they had entered into defensive military alliances which they felt bound to honour. The first of these was the Triple Alliance, forged by an earlier German Chancellor, Otto von Bismarck. Germany had inflicted a decisive defeat on France in 1871 in the last of the wars which created the German Empire. Bismarck wanted to prevent the French from taking revenge for this defeat and for Germany's annexation of their valuable provinces, Alsace and Lorraine. Thus he negotiated treaties with Austria (1879) and Italy (1882), depriving France of potential allies. The Triple Alliance was also directed against Russia, which contended with Austria for control in the Balkans (South Eastern Europe). But the wily Chancellor also managed to keep Russia friendly by means of the so-called Reinsurance Treaty (1887).

After William II dismissed Bismarck in 1890 the diplomatic situation changed dramatically. In spite of his close family ties with the Tsar, the new Kaiser thought that friendship with Russia might stand in the way of German ambitions and he refused to renew the Reinsurance Treaty. An unlikely partnership was then formed in 1894 between republican France and autocratic Russia, sustained by their common fear of the Central Powers (Germany, Austria and Italy) as well as by heavy French investment in the Russian economy. Germany was now less secure since, if war broke out, it would have powerful enemies on both sides.

Britain at this point remained in the 'splendid isolation' prized during the 1880s when it had the strongest navy, the most prosperous economy and the largest empire in the world. By the early twentieth century, however, several factors had sapped British confidence. Defeating the Boers in South Africa (1899–1902) had proved unexpectedly difficult; America and Germany were now outstripping Britain's industrial production; and, most ominously, in 1898 Germany had launched a ship building programme which threatened British naval supremacy. An alliance with Japan in 1902 reduced Britain's naval commitment in the Pacific Ocean. Two years later

Britain entered into the *Entente Cordiale* with its traditional enemy France. This was not a military alliance, but Britain secretly promised to support French claims to the independent North African state of Morocco in return for French recognition of British rule in Egypt. Britain signed a similar agreement with another former foe, Russia, in 1907 thus creating a Triple Entente and infuriating the Kaiser, who accused his uncle King Edward VII of 'encircling' Germany.

Liberal academics, such as G. Lowes Dickinson in *The International Anarchy* (1926), believed that this devious and often secret diplomacy was responsible for the atmosphere of mistrust and hostility which led to war. It is true that countries were drawn into war by their mutual commitments and by the military plans that followed from them. However, armed camps in themselves do not necessarily cause wars: indeed, the mutual fear they engender can preserve peace. Leaders decide what course of action suits their countries' interests at a given time. Thus the Italian Prime Minister declared on 1 August 1914 that Italy was not obliged to back Austria and Germany in a conflict over the Balkans which he did not consider to be 'a war of defence'. Grey, on the other hand, allowed Britain to become militarily involved without being bound by any treaty. It has been argued, too, that Germany's unconditional promise of support to Austria and rapid declaration of war on France and Russia far exceeded its treaty obligations – which could only mean that Germany wanted a European war.[10]

b) Economic and Imperial Rivalry

One of the earliest interpretations of the 1914 crisis was that given by the Russian Communist leader, Lenin. In his pamphlet *Imperialism – The Highest Form of Capitalism* (1916) he argued that capitalist countries were bound to engage in competition for new markets and fields of investment. Imperial rivalry would inevitably lead to war among 'powerful world plunderers armed to the teeth'.[11] Lenin's idea was taken up by Marxist historians and still contributes to our understanding of the causes of the war and of its global nature.

In the late nineteenth century most of Africa and much of Asia had fallen under European rule or 'protection'. The grab for empire was largely inspired by economic interests, though European nations also aimed to enhance their power and prestige. Some felt, too, that they were taking up what Kipling called 'The White Man's Burden' – bringing civilisation to subject peoples. There was also an element of manly adventure in these far-flung conquests, which made them popular at home. Britain and France acquired the largest empires and they nearly came to blows on several occasions before making up their differences in 1904.

Two other Great Powers, Austria–Hungary and Russia, controlled older empires in Europe itself (though Russia's enormous land mass straddled Asia as well). Both aimed at expansion in the Balkans, the largely Slav region of south-eastern Europe, parts of which still belonged to the declining Ottoman (Turkish) Empire. Austria particularly wanted to gain more Adriatic coastline while Russia's dream was to control Constantinople, the gateway to the Dardanelles Straits and thence to the Mediterranean. Both, too, feared that their existing empires would disintegrate if the many different ethnic groups under their sway intensified their demands for self-government.

Europe's newest nations, Italy and Germany, considered themselves cheated in the imperial stakes and demanded their 'place in the sun'. Italy's burning ambition to establish its Great Power status by acquiring a Mediterranean empire was one of its motives for joining the Triple Alliance. Germany's *Weltpolitik* (policy of world expansion) challenged especially the British claim to be 'the greatest of governing races that the world has ever seen'.[12] Since Britain, already envious of Germany's industrial might, was determined to maintain its imperial supremacy, Anglo-German conflict was a real possibility. Britain was suspicious, for instance, about the German project for building a railway from Berlin via Constantinople to Baghdad; yet the British decision in 1914 to invest in the scheme after all suggests that cooperation was possible.

While imperial friction did not necessarily lead to fighting there was always that danger and it certainly helped to kindle the crisis of 1914. Austria's arrogant treatment in that year of the 'mischief-making' Slavs inside its empire and on its borders has been likened to Britain's behaviour towards its colonial subjects.[13] Such attitudes helped to precipitate the First World War and for this all the major powers must bear some blame.

c) Crises 1905–13

These hostile alliances and imperial rivalries were both at work in the crises which imperilled Europe in pre-war years. Germany first tested the strength of the Anglo-French Entente in 1905, when the Kaiser interrupted a Mediterranean cruise to land at the Moroccan port of Tangier. He made a speech there supporting the independence of Morocco and thus challenged French claims. At the ensuing Algeçiras Conference, Britain upheld France's right to intervene in Moroccan affairs and the Entente partners went on to hold secret military 'conversations', no record of which was kept. Only Austria, now an indispensable ally, backed German interests.

The mutual dependence of these two Central Powers was further shown in 1908 when unrest in Turkey gave Austria the opportunity to take into its empire the two Balkan provinces of Bosnia and Herzegovina (over which it had previously had only administrative rights). This led to talk of war between Austria and Russia, until the Kaiser demanded that Russia accept the annexation. Still weak after being defeated in the Russo-Japanese War (1904–5) and lacking support from France and Britain, Russia had to back down. Russian Slavophiles were determined that such a humiliation should not happen again.

The year 1911 saw another war scare when a German gunboat appeared at the Moroccan port of Agadir to protest against the presence of French troops in the country. Britain regarded the vessel as a threat to its own 'national honour' (the words used by the normally pacific Liberal, Lloyd George) and gave strong diplomatic support to France. Germany, which did not have even Austrian backing this time, was obliged to recognise most of Morocco as a French protectorate (the northern coastline being awarded to Spain) and to content itself with compensatory strips of land in the French Congo. A greater threat to German interests was the secret naval agreement which now gave teeth to the *Entente Cordiale*: British ships were to safeguard the Channel and the North Sea (where Germany's growing fleet was concentrated), allowing the French to move their vessels to the Mediterranean.

In the midst of the Agadir Crisis Italy took advantage of the Ottoman Empire's continuing weakness to occupy the Turkish North African province of Libya. The qualms of Italy's Prime Minister, Giovanni Giolitti, about this imperialist venture are suggested in his prediction of its possible consequences:

1　The integrity of what remains of the Ottoman Empire is one of the principles on which the equilibrium and peace of Europe is based ... Can it be in the interests of Italy to shatter one of the cornerstones of the old edifice? And what if after we have attacked Turkey, the Balkans begin
5　to stir? And what if a Balkan war provokes a clash between the two power blocs and a European war? Can it be that we can shoulder the responsibility of putting a match to the powder?[14]

This speech, made in April 1911, proved remarkably prophetic; and it also lends weight to the idea of collective guilt. The Balkans did begin to 'stir' after this. Under Russia's protective eye, Serbia, Bulgaria, Montenegro and Greece formed a Balkan League which declared war on the Ottoman Empire in 1912. All four countries gained territory from Turkey but it was Serbia which benefited most. In the subsequent Balkan war of 1913, provoked by a jealous Bulgaria, Serbia acquired even more land – though not the coastline it craved. This ambitious Slav state was now perceived by Austria as a serious threat to its imperial interests. Germany used Turkey's defeat as a pretext for sending a military mission under General Liman von Sanders to advise on the modernisation of the Turkish army. Despite objections from Russia, the General was still in Constantinople at the outbreak of war.

Up to this point, however, the Balkan wars had not provoked the 'clash between the two power blocs' predicted by Giolitti. In fact Grey was able to assemble the ambassadors of the Great Powers at the London Conference to settle the conflict. Winston Churchill (then Britain's First Lord of the Admiralty) was to recall: 'The spring and summer of 1914 were marked by an exceptional tranquillity.'[15] One reason for this, it seems, was that neither Russia nor Germany had completed its military preparations.

d) The Arms Race

In Bernard Shaw's play *Major Barbara*, Andrew Undershaft describes himself as an unashamed 'profiteer in mutilation and murder'; he is pleased to have invented a new gun which 'blew twenty-seven dummy soldiers into fragments'. To the comforting argument that 'the more destructive war becomes, the sooner it will be abolished', he replies honestly: 'The more destructive war becomes the more fascinating we find it.'[16] This controversy is as relevant today as it was in 1905, when industry was producing ever more sophisticated artillery, machine-guns, torpedoes, grenades, mortars, battleships and aircraft. As countries competed to build up their stocks of such weapons, firms like Nobel, Vickers, Krupp, Skoda and Creusot grew rich by selling their wares to anyone who would buy them, including rival governments. It would be an over-simplification to suggest that such economic interests caused the world war, but they encouraged a war spirit and they certainly made the fighting more deadly.

Another aspect of the arms race was the building up of large forces. Most European countries adopted some form of compulsory military service, though this was not always popular. In France, for instance, there was such resistance to government plans to increase conscription from two to three years that the change had not been implemented when war began. The multinational Austro-Hungarian army was plagued by bitter disputes. Russia's peasant conscripts were loath to leave their villages. Successive British governments refused to risk votes by introducing national service, despite pressure from men like Kipling. Military service was probably accepted most readily in Germany, where the army enjoyed enormous influence and respect. But all the Great Powers (except Britain) knew that millions of trained servicemen and reserves could be quickly mobilised – as indeed happened in July–August 1914.

The development which had most serious repercussions was that of the German navy. Admiral Tirpitz introduced his first Naval Laws in 1898 and 1900, ordering the building of 55 new battleships. In response Britain's Admiral Fisher pioneered the Dreadnought, a larger, faster, more expensive, better-armed vessel than any of its predecessors. The race was now on between Britain and Germany (and the other naval powers) to build more Dreadnoughts as well as submarines and ordinary battleships. In 1914 Britain was still in the lead (with 29 Dreadnoughts to Germany's 17)[17] and furthermore it had made alliances and strategic agreements to counter the German naval challenge. The launching of new ships, the taxes which they required, the creation of bigger harbours and the widening of Germany's Kiel Canal (not completed until June 1914) could not escape public attention. Newspaper articles, posters, slogans, Navy Leagues, reviews of the fleet and even children in sailor suits stirred up an aggressive climate of public opinion in both Britain and Germany. A novel commissioned by the *Daily Mail* scared the British public with its depiction of *The Invasion of 1910*; a popular German rhyme expressed 'hate by water and hate by land' towards the 'foe – England'. Militarism had created an atmosphere fraught with tension and danger.

e) Battle Plans

Much less obvious to the people of Europe were the secret battle plans made in their name by military chiefs. Germany's plan, devised by Chief of Staff General Schlieffen in the 1890s and modified by his successor, General Moltke, was designed to avoid fighting on two fronts. A lightning attack on France through Belgium would knock out that enemy before the Russians could get their troops to Germany's eastern frontier. Belgium's neutrality, guaranteed since 1839 by most European countries (including Germany), was a complication of little concern to the German army, which was free from civilian control. Under Moltke's direction the Schlieffen Plan was put in train immediately after Germany's declaration of war on Russia and clearly helped to make this a general war. Austro-Hungarian plans were less precise; their obsession with Serbia required an immediate attack southwards, but it was not entirely clear how troops would also be able to engage with the Russians on the northern frontier.

Both the Central Powers assumed that Russia could not move its huge army across its vast country within 30 days. In fact, with French advice and loans, Russia had greatly improved its railway system and army since the Russo-Japanese war. By 1914 plans were ready for speedy mobilisation against both Austria-Hungary and Germany, threatening the viability of the Schlieffen Plan. Secure in his knowledge of Russian plans (but lacking accurate intelligence of German strategy), Joffre had devised Plan XVII for an all-out French attack on Alsace-Lorraine. But civilian authority was paramount in France and Poincaré would not allow Joffre to move troops within ten kilometres of the German frontier until war had been declared.

Even the British Expeditionary Force, new and small though it was, had plans for a swift intervention in the event of a German attack on Belgium and France. As it happened, though, the British navy was probably better prepared than any other force, since Churchill ordered it to stay at sea after the Grand Review of the Fleet on 17–18 July. As he wrote later: 'They were going on a longer voyage than any of us could know.'[18]

The speed with which military plans had to be implemented precipitated many of the fateful decisions of 1914: the mobilisation of Austria against Serbia on 25 July, of Russia against Austria and Germany on 30 July and of Germany against France on 31 July. It was difficult (though not impossible) to call a halt once hundreds of thousands of soldiers were on the move.

f) Public Opinion

News of the war was greeted with enthusiasm throughout Europe. Anxious not to miss the action, young men rushed to the colours. They did not wait to be called up but volunteered to fight for Holy Russia, Britannia, *La Patrie* and the *Vaterland*.

> Now, God be thanked Who has matched us with His hour,
> And caught our youth, and wakened us from sleeping.[19]

Evidence abounds that young men everywhere shared Rupert Brooke's view of war as a liberating experience. It was 'a challenge', as J.B. Priestley said, to their 'untested manhood'. Many years of patriotic education combined with the recent war scares, luridly reported in the popular press, to create the 'mood of 1914'. In addition, each government took great care to justify its involvement.

The unity created by war was naturally welcomed by European governments, all of which had faced domestic conflict in the pre-war years. For a time at least, British trade unionists, suffragettes and Ulstermen, national groups within Austria-Hungary, French anti-militarists, German socialists and even some Russian revolutionaries (though not Lenin's followers) put aside their grievances. It cannot be proved that leaders (even in Germany) cynically sought war as a solution to their domestic troubles. But they were not slow to take advantage of the bellicose mentality of 1914.

The question which remains is that raised by Kipling's couplet: were the older men who held political and the military power deceiving the young men who went off to defend honourable patriotic causes? Austria-Hungary claimed to be defending its empire against the threat of Slav nationalism; but this amounted to the arrogant bullying of a smaller neighbour. Russia was ostensibly protecting the Slavs from domination by Austria-Hungary and Germany while at the same time furthering its own Balkan ambitions. France professed to be fighting an aggressive neighbour; but it was gladly taking the opportunity to avenge the defeat of 1871. Britain proudly maintained that it was defending gallant little Belgium; but its own naval and imperial supremacy was also at stake. Germany declared that it was supporting an ally and acting in self-defence; yet it also sought war to assert itself as a world power.

All the belligerents except Germany were aiming to uphold their existing world status, 'won by centuries of heroism and achievement'.

But Germany's new, impatient *Weltpolitik* had upset the balance of power and can, to that extent, be blamed for causing the First World War.

5 Looking Ahead

> **KEY ISSUE** Why was the war fought on such a wide scale and for such a long time?

By the end of 1914 men were fighting not only in Serbia where the war started but in Belgium, Northern France, Eastern Germany, the borderlands of Austria-Hungary and Russia, Germany's African colonies and on the high seas. As more countries became involved, the scale of the conflict widened still further and people began to refer to this as the Great War. Turkey's entry on the side of the Central Powers in October led to fighting in the Arab lands of the Ottoman Empire. Japan's willingness to honour its 1902 alliance with Britain engendered conflict in the Pacific and the Far East. After April 1915 when Italy decided to join France, Britain and Russia (which will now be referred to as the Allies) a new front was opened in Northern Italy. The Balkans became more heavily involved when Bulgaria joined the Central Powers in October 1915 and Romania the Allies in August 1916.

The illusion of a short war had long been shattered by this time and no end was in sight. Chapters 3, 4 and 5 will describe the various areas of conflict and discuss the factors most likely to determine its outcome. Could Germany overcome the combined weight of its western and eastern foes? Would Britain's superior navy, so keenly coveted by Germany, enable it to scatter its enemies? Or would the war be decided in the imperial arena of Africa or Asia? How much would depend on civilians' contribution to a conflict so greedy for men and munitions?

As chapter 6 will demonstrate, two decisions in 1917 changed the course of the war: that of America's President Woodrow Wilson to engage on the side of the Allies and that of Russia's new Communist government to sign an armistice. Each side had gained an advantage which it thought would lead to victory. Not until the autumn of 1918 was it clear whose assumptions were correct; indeed many Germans claimed for long afterwards that their country was not actually defeated on the battlefield in November 1918. Chapters 7 and 8 will deal with the many spheres of life touched by these four years of total war, suggesting that it is difficult to understand the twentieth century without a knowledge of the First World War.

References

1 R. Kipling, 'Common Form' quoted in *Complete Verse* (CUP, 1990), p. 314.
2 D. Lloyd George, *War Memoirs* (Odhams Press, 1938), Vol. I, p. 32.
3 L. Albertini, *Origins of the War of 1914*, trans. I. Massey (OUP, 1957), Vol. II, p. 136.
4 F. Fischer, *World Power or Decline: The Controversy over Germany's Aims in the First World War* (Norton & Co., 1974), p. xvii.
5 I. Geiss (ed.), *July 1914: The Outbreak of the First World War: Selected Documents* (Norton & Co., 1965), p. 77.
6 G.P. Gooch & H. Temperley, *British Documents on the Origins of the War* (H.M.S.O., 1929), Vol. XI, p. 73.
7 K. Wilson (ed.), *Decisions for War 1914* (UCL Press, 1995), p. 140.
8 H. Herwig, *The First World War: Germany and Austria-Hungary 1914–1918* (Arnold, 1997), p. 18.
9 A.C. Morales, *Europe: The Last Hundred Years* (Macmillan, 1979), p. 31.
10 See, for example, J. Röhl in Wilson, *Decisions for War*, p. 28 ff.
11 J. Watson, *European History 1815–1941* (John Murray, 1981), p. 254.
12 Speech of Joseph Chamberlain (Colonial Secretary) in 1895 in J. Joll, *The Origins of the First World War* (Longman, 1984), p. 150.
13 F. Fellner in Wilson, *Decisions for War*, p. 14.
14 Joll, *Origins of the First World War*, p. 164.
15 W. Churchill, *The World Crisis: 1911–1918* (Odhams Press, 1938), Vol. I, p. 143.
16 G.B. Shaw, *Major Barbara*, (Penguin, 1957), p. 70.
17 N. Ferguson, *The Pity of War* (Allen Lane, 1998), p. 85.
18 Churchill, *World Crisis*, Vol. I, p. 153.
19 R. Brooke, 'Peace' in B. Gardner, *Up the Line to Death* (Methuen, 1976), p. 10.

Summary Diagram

The Different Spheres of Action in the First World War

	New participants	Western Front and Italy	Eastern Front	Sea and Air	Africa and Asia
1914	Japan (Allies) Turkey (Central Powers)	German invasion of Belgium Fall of Brussels Battle of Mons Battle of the Marne Battle of Ypres (1) Christmas 'truce'	Austrian invasion of Serbia Russian invasion of Germany and Battles of Tannenburg and Masurian Lakes Austrian invasion of Russia Battle of Lemburg	British blockade Battles of Heligoland, Falkland Islands and Coronel	Conquest of German Togoland and possessions in Pacific
1915	Italy (Allies) Bulgaria (Central Powers)	Trench warfare Battle of Neuve Chapelle Battle of Ypres (2) Battle of Loos Battles on the Isonzo (Italy)	Defeat of Serbia Gallipoli campaign Defeat of Russia in Galicia	Submarine warfare Sinking of Lusitania Battle of Dogger Bank Zeppelin raid on Britain	Conquest of German S.W. Africa
1916	Portugal Romania (Allies)	Battle of Verdun Battle of the Somme Battles on the Isonzo and in Dolomites	End of Gallipoli campaign Brusilov offensive on Austria	Battle of Jutland	Arab revolt in Turkey Surrender of German Cameroon
1917	U.S.A. Greece (Allies)	Nivelle offensive French mutinies Battles of Vimy Ridge and Arras Battle of Ypres (3) Battle of Cambrai Battle of Caporetto (Italy)	Overthrow of Tsar in Russia Communist revolution in Russia Russian armistice	Unrestricted submarine warfare British convoy system	British capture of Kut and Baghdad Allenby's desert campaign Capture of Jerusalem
1918		Ludendorff offensive Arrival of American troops Allied counter-offensive Battle of Vittorio Veneto (Italy) Abdication of Kaiser Surrender of Germany	Treaty of Brest Litovsk Surrender of Bulgaria, Turkey and Austria	British attack on Zeebrugge Naval mutiny in Germany	Capture of Damascus

2 The Belligerents' Aims and Resources 1914–1917

POINTS TO CONSIDER

It is important while reading this chapter to refer constantly to the table on page 16, using it to compare the military and economic resources of the two sides at the outbreak of war. The aims of the belligerent powers were vague, flexible, conflicting and often secret. Thus they cannot be presented in a simple and straightforward form.

KEY DATES

1914 Japanese declaration of war on Germany
Proclamation of Germany's September Programme
Turkish declaration of war on the Allies
Publication of French war aims
1915 Allied recognition of Russian aims in Dardanelles
Treaty of London between Italy and the Allies
Italian declaration of war on Austria
Bulgarian declaration of war on the Allies
1916 Austrian plans for expansion in Balkans
Allied recognition of Russia's plans for Poland
Sykes-Picot agreement for Allied partition of Arab lands
Italian declaration of war on Germany
Portugal and Romania join the Allies
1917 Allied recognition of Japanese claims in Pacific
President Wilson's 14 Points
American declaration of war on Germany

1 Introduction

'War is a continuation of politics by other means', wrote the nineteenth-century military theorist Karl von Clausewitz. Politicians did, indeed, resort to war in August 1914 in the interests of their countries. They also negotiated with other governments to widen the conflict and they sustained it over a period of four years. While men killed each other in the muddy trenches of Flanders, on the bleak plains of Eastern Europe, among the cloudy mountain-tops of Italy, in the deserts of Arabia, in the bush of East Africa, in the air and on the oceans, statesmen and diplomats conferred about the desired fruits of victory. From time to time governments sought to justify the prolonged fighting by making announcements about the war aims which they had belatedly formulated. It was safer to keep quiet about them, however, since they were often muddled and incompatible with the aspirations of allies. This chapter explores the declared and secret aims of the major combatant countries between 1914 and 1917. It also examines the means with which they hoped to achieve them, comparing the two sides and considering the extent to which the result of the war was determined by their initial resources.

	Germany	Austria/ Hungary	Turkey	Britain	France	Russia	Japan	Italy	USA
Population (mill)	65	52	21	45	39	171	55	37	98
Naval/military personnel (peace time strength) (thous)	891	444	240?	532	910	1352	306	345	164
Army after mobilisation (mill)	4.5	3	2	1 (inc. Empire)	4	5.9		1.25 (1915)	
Warship tonnage (thous)	1305	372		2714	900	679	700	498	985
Aircraft	200	84		95	200	360		115	
Defence Expenditure (£ mill)	117.8	42.4		75.7	65.9	101.8		39.6	
Iron/steel production (mill tons)	17.6	2.6		7.7	4.6	4.8	0.25	0.93	31.8
Wheat production (thous tons)	4343	4240		1772	7690	68864		4493	
% of world's manufacturing output	14.8	4.4		13.6	6.1	8.2		2.4	32

Central Powers   Allies   Neutral

Table: The Resources of the Major Powers at the Start of War[1]

2 The Central Powers

KEY ISSUE How adequate were the resources of the Central Powers for the achievement of their ambitions?

a) Germany

With its substantial, well-trained army, large body of trained reservists, powerful battle fleet, plentiful artillery and developing air power, Germany embarked on the war with confidence and did not think it necessary to plan for the use of colonial troops. Its striking military assets were backed up by a productive agriculture, manufacturing industries second only to those of the USA, a good communications system and a fast-growing population. All this made Germany a formidable enemy. Even in this efficient state, however, 'there were no plans whatsoever' for a protracted war.[2] It was not clear how Germany's undemocratic and bureaucratic government would be able to supply its troops, feed the population and pay the bills over a long period. Nor was it certain that the euphoric patriotism of 1914 would continue to mask the political, religious and regional divisions which 43 years of Imperial Germany's existence had failed to remove. German hopes were therefore placed on the quick victory which the Schlieffen Plan seemed to promise (see page 10).

There was evidently much support in 1914 for the ambitious war aims first formulated during the autumn in Bethmann Hollweg's controversial 'September Programme' and in subsequent memoranda from other political and military leaders. These demanded the formation of a central European customs and economic union led by Germany and Austria-Hungary, to be known as *Mitteleuropa*. This would involve the annexation of Luxemburg and possibly some of France, the control of Belgium and the acquisition of its Channel ports, and the release from Russian rule of the Baltic states and Poland, which would then come under German 'influence'. An equivalent scheme would create hegemony in Africa – *Mittelafrika*. Military leaders tended to make larger claims than the Chancellor but all apparently agreed that Germany should expand its overseas empire and dominate Europe. Since public discussion of war aims was soon forbidden, it is difficult to judge how far the German people supported these grandiose ambitions. There was a right-wing War Aims Movement which wanted still more, while many socialists favoured more restraint. Anyway, the aims remained in place, stiffening Allied resistance to 'German militarism' and thus helping to prolong the war.

b) The Austro-Hungarian Empire

In spite of its long history and impressive size, the Empire was the weaker partner in its alliance with Germany. It was not therefore in a position to object to German war aims, even though some of them conflicted with imperial interests; the proposed 'liberation' of Russian Poland, for instance, might cause unrest among Austria's eight million Polish subjects. The Empire's other ethnic groups also gave cause for concern: with Slavs (who made up 46 per cent of the population), Czechs, Romanians and Italians asserting their national rights it was not even certain that the Imperial army (where orders had to be given in as many as 15 languages) would remain loyal under the strain of war. In addition, low pre-war defence spending meant that the army was poorly equipped while the navy was the smallest in Europe. Low iron and steel production meant that these deficiencies could not easily be made good. By 1916, these inadequate forces faced enemies on all sides: Serbia and Romania to the south-east, Italy to the south-west and Russia to the north-east. The Empire's greatest strength was the German alliance.

'We were bound to die,' lamented the Austrian Foreign Minister after the war. Yet the Empire had aimed not just at survival but at expansion in the Balkans. The government announced plans in January 1916 to make Albania a Habsburg protectorate, to annex half of Serbia and to take over Montenegro's coastline. From Italy Vienna claimed only frontier adjustments. But an Italian soldier remembers Austrian troops in 1916 shouting with avaricious excitement as they viewed from a Dolomite peak 'the shining pearls of the Venetian plain ... Verona, Vicenza, Treviso, Padua. And in the distance to the left, Venice. Venice!'[3]

c) Turkey

The Muslim state of Turkey signed a secret alliance with the Central Powers on 2 August 1914. The Kaiser had for long cultivated this friendship, even though Turkey was known as 'the sick man of Europe' on account of its corrupt and often cruel Sultanate, its unsuccessful, ill-equipped army and its almost non-existent navy. Nothing better illustrates the ineptitude of the regime than the fact that Sultan Abdul Hamid the Damned ordered Turkey's few good foreign-built ships to be dismantled in case they should be used against him. By 1914, however, Abdul had been deposed and his brother forced to share power with the revolutionary Young Turk Movement, which was rather more modern in outlook though no less autocratic. By this time, too, German advice and money were beginning to bring about some military improvements. The size of the army mobilised in October 1914, when Turkey declared war on the Allies, is difficult to estimate; but, in the opinion of a recent historian, the theoretical 'establishment of 17,000 officers and a quarter of a million other ranks was never remotely approached'.[4] Christians and Jews were conscripted but were only allowed to serve in labour battalions.

Largely because of its geographical position, Turkey caused serious problems for the Allies. Even before its official declaration of war Turkey complied with German wishes that the fortifications on the Dardanelles should be directed against Allied shipping. Once hostilities began Russia had to divert troops southwards to fight in the Caucasus, where Turkey wanted to regain territory lost in earlier wars. This was one of its chief war aims. It also dreamt of recapturing Egypt and Cyprus from Britain. The Turkish government announced that theirs was a holy war (*jihad*) and backed up the claim with far-fetched assertions that the Kaiser was a Muslim whose family was descended from Mohammed's sister.[5]

Turkey also wanted to reoccupy land lost to its former Balkan possessions. But this aspiration became an embarrassment after 1915 when one of them (Bulgaria) was induced to join the Central Powers by promises of extra territory.

3 The Allies

> **KEY ISSUES** Were the combined resources of the Allies sufficient to ensure victory over the Central Powers and to achieve their own aims?

a) Britain and its Empire

Conscious though many Edwardian Britons were of decline, their country still possessed great assets, some of which had actually been improved under the spur of adversity. German competition had stimulated expansion of the British navy, though it still could not completely protect the far-flung empire. Unexpected set-backs during the Boer war at the turn of the century had inspired reforms in the regular army, which remained small but was now a little more efficient and better equipped. It is true that the challenge posed by Germany and the USA had not led to industrial modernisation, except in shipbuilding, but Britain was still a wealthy trading nation and the City of London was the financial capital of the world. These were to prove invaluable assets in this costly war.

One reason for this wealth was Britain's empire, which included a quarter of the world's population. It served as a market for manufactured goods, an outlet for capital investment and a source of raw materials. Another boon for the 'Mother Country' was the availability of colonial troops in time of war. They made an important contribution, particularly in view of Britain's reluctance to introduce conscription. As early as September 1914 four Indian divisions arrived on the Western Front to fight in that first winter, suffering high casualties in the unfamiliar climate as well as in battle. Nearly one and a half million Indian volunteers served in the British army during the war, on the Western Front until 1915 and then in Mesopotamia in the Middle East. The self-governing Dominions (Canada, Australia, New Zealand and South Africa) contributed well over one million servicemen, who fought in France, Belgium, Turkey and Africa. The South African regiments on the Western Front included the 'Native Labour Contingent' of black troops who did vital work in transporting supplies, digging trenches and clearing land. Half a million locally recruited troops served in Africa itself. The West Indian colonies quickly offered their patriotic support for the mother-country but War Secretary Lord Kitchener reflected the prejudices of his day in worrying that black troops would be 'conspicuous on the battlefield', giving the impression that Britain was resorting to the 'dregs of humanity'. Only with the shortage of manpower in 1915 were black West Indian volunteers accepted on the Western Front but they were never used as more than labour battalions. For them 'it was a heart-breaking tale of humiliation and disillusion', according to their white officer Colonel Wood-Hill.[6] But for Britain, over a third of whose manpower was non-white, the colonial contribution was vital.

As far as war aims were concerned, Britain did not admit to wanting more territory. Political speeches in 1914 referred to those goals which had brought it into the war: maintaining naval supremacy, restoring Belgium to its independent status and 'smashing Prussian militarism' – though there were differing views on how the last aim should be achieved. Over the next two years Britain's dependence on its Dominions and Allies, as well as its own enduring imperial ambitions, gave rise to new secret arrangements. Australia and New Zealand were promised permanent possession of the German South Pacific islands they had occupied and a similar pledge was made to South Africa regarding German South-West Africa. Canada was the only Dominion not to be offered a reward for its loyalty. Mere colonies did not need to be compensated.

Italy and Japan were offered Austrian and German lands in return for their support (see pages 22–23). In the Sykes-Picot agreement of 1916 British and French diplomats secretly carved up Turkey's Asiatic empire. Britain was to gain control in Mesopotamia and France in Lebanon and Syria. Italy and Russia were allocated 'areas of control' on the Middle Eastern map. As David Stevenson writes, 'The drive to annex and establish spheres of influence was not a purely German sickness.'[7] To encourage revolt among Turkey's Arab subjects, Sykes-Picot also proposed an independent Confederation of Arab States in which Britain and France would have certain 'rights'.

b) France and its Empire

France had recovered quickly from its defeat by Germany in 1871. Since then it had acquired allies and colonies, invested lavishly abroad (especially in Russia), built up a large army and a useful fleet. Nevertheless, France had cause to fear Germany. French industry had developed fast but it was much less productive than that of its prosperous neighbour. One reason for this was that France lacked essential natural resources like iron and coal, a disadvantage accentuated by the loss of Alsace and Lorraine and by the German occupation of its northern industrial areas throughout the war. Another resource which France lacked was people; for reasons which remain unclear its population growth was far outstripped by Germany's. Thus to make up its large army the French government had to recruit about 80 per cent of the men in the relevant age group (compared to 50 per cent in Germany); it also depended heavily on 600,000 colonial troops from North and West Africa and French Indo-China (Vietnam, Cambodia and Laos). France went into battle in 1914 united and confident of victory. But, as the war dragged on, its relative lack of economic and human resources became an increasing disadvantage.

France intended to make good its national deficiencies, as was made clear in its war aims published in December 1914. But, here too, allies found themselves at odds, since French aspirations did not prove wholly acceptable to Britain. Even the recovery of Alsace and Lorraine, which the French government regarded as essential, was not fully supported by Britain (or by French socialists) because of uncertainty about whether the inhabitants wished to be French or German. On the restoration of Belgium, the allies were united; but France would not join Britain in encouraging the Belgian claim to Luxemburg, secretly coveting this region for itself. About getting compensation and ending German militarism there was further disagreement. Even in the early stages of the war, France envisaged annexation of, or the creation of buffer states in, the Rhineland border areas, an idea unacceptable to Britain. These disputes were still unresolved at the end of the war and were to cause fierce arguments at the Versailles Peace Conference. On the division of spoils in the Middle East, however, there was cordial agreement among all the Entente governments.

c) Russia

To its enemies the imminent advance of the 'Russian bear' or the 'Russian steam-roller' was a frightening prospect. With its ever-expanding territory, fast-growing population and huge army, it overshadowed any other Great Power. It is true that none of these assets had saved Russia from defeat by its small eastern neighbour, Japan, in 1905 but that humiliation had proved salutary. Since then there had been some political reform, unprecedented economic growth and improvements in its armed forces sufficient to cause alarm in Germany.

But Russia's strengths were not always as impressive as they seemed to foreign observers. The new *Duma* (Parliament) had very little power and gave only a frustrating taste of democracy. The large empire contained many nationalities which had no wish to be ruled by Russia. Most of the people did not share in the increasing prosperity of the country and remained miserably poor; this applied both to the 80 per cent who were still peasants and to those who congregated in the growing cities. These grievances combined to

produce a proliferation of revolutionary groups in the early twentieth century. Thus the armies which went off to fight for the Tsar in
1914 included large numbers of illiterate peasants, resentful ethnic
minorities and Communist workers eager to use the armed forces as
their own recruiting ground. This was to prove a dangerous mixture
(see pages 56–57). There were further deficiencies in the Russian
steam-roller. Artillery tended to be placed in fortresses rather than
at the battlefield; the army was split between the German and the
Austrian frontiers; and the new railway system was overloaded with
horses for the cavalry in which army commanders still placed their
faith. Norman Stone's ironic conclusion is that 'the sacrifice of loco-
motives to horses was a suitable way for this army to enter the war in
1914'.[8]

Like its allies, Russia was confident that victory would bring its
rewards. One long-held aspiration was that of uniting the Polish
people (divided between Germany, Austria and Russia before the
war) 'under the sceptre of the Russian Empire, free in faith, language
and self-government'.[9] In November 1916 France and Britain reluctantly agreed to this scheme in order to keep Russia in the war.
Another Russian aim was the annexation of Constantinople and of
the European and Asian shores of the Dardanelles; the allies backed
this in March 1915 at the time of the Gallipoli campaign (see pages
57–60). Things had changed since the 1870s when a British popular
song swore that 'by jingo ... while Britons shall be true, The Russians
shall not have Constantinople'.

d) Italy

Italy's diplomatic *volte-faces* were even more extraordinary. Having
benefited from French military help when expelling Austria from
northern Italy during Italian unification in the 1860s, it later joined
the Austro-German alliance which was directed against France. But
in 1914 Italy was too busy subduing Libya and too worried about
Austrian expansion in the Balkans to join the Central Powers. A
vociferous minority felt dishonoured by Italian neutrality – though
most people were probably thankful not to have to fight. The conservative government of the day, led by Antonio Salandra, was
pledged to a policy of *sacro egoismo*: it would do whatever was in
Italy's best interests. Negotiations with both sides during 1914–15
convinced him and his Foreign Minister that more was to be
gained by intervening on the side of the Allies. They were promised
not only the northern regions of Trentino and South Tyrol, coveted ever since unification, but also the port of Trieste, Istria and
half of the Dalmatian coast, which would give Italy control of the
Adriatic. There was no talk of holding plebiscites to determine the
wishes of the people in these regions, who spoke a variety of languages. A share of Germany's African colonies was also part of the

deal. On 26 April 1915, without consulting army leaders or members of parliament, Salandra signed the Treaty of London. A month later Italy declared war on Austria-Hungary, though not on Germany until August 1916. Most Socialists and Catholics (probably most Italians, in fact) had wanted Italy to remain neutral. Certainly the country was not swept into war by the tide of popular demand later evoked by nationalists like Benito Mussolini and Gabriele d'Annunzio.

So there was no doubt about Italy's war aims and its leaders were as confident as those of any other belligerent country about achieving them. Italy had the fastest rate of economic growth in Europe and firms like Fiat and Pirelli were only too willing to supply the forces with armaments and vehicles. But its dependence on coal imports (mainly from Britain) and its backward agriculture would cause problems of supply as the fighting continued. There were financial difficulties too, since huge debts had already been incurred by the Libyan war. The Italian army was a respectable size but it was not 'a nation in arms'; Martin Clark describes it rather as 'a sullen, often illiterate, ill-equipped army, torn away from its homes and fields to fight on foreign soil for incomprehensible reasons'.[10] The lack of enthusiasm was accentuated by the fact that most front-line troops came from the poverty-stricken south, which had never been fully integrated into the Italian nation.

Nevertheless the Allies valued Italy's intervention. It kept Austrian divisions pinned down in the Isonzo area and the Dolomites, making the Empire even more dependent on German help in fighting Russia. Also the Italian navy prevented Austrian ships from leaving the Adriatic and later attacked German vessels in the Mediterranean.

e) Japan

Japan had become a Great Power as a result of its rapid industrial development and modernisation since 1890, but its defeat of Russia in 1905 had still taken the world by surprise. In 1914 its well-trained army (full of *samurai* spirit) and impressive navy made it a powerful foe. Britain was worried, however, when Japan declared war on Germany on 23 August, that its alacrity was due to expansionist aims in the Far East – the 'yellow peril' might threaten the empire which coloured so much of the global map red. British fears were confirmed in 1915 when Japan presented its 'Twenty-One Demands' to China after a successful Anglo-Japanese attack on the German province of Kiaochow on the Chinese coast. If accepted, these would have given Japan control over Chinese economic and political affairs. Eventually the Japanese government was persuaded to modify its demands and in 1917 the Allies formally recognised its claims to the German Pacific islands which it had occupied and to German trading rights in Kiaochow.

4 Conclusion

> **KEY ISSUE** What factors other than military and economic resources might affect the outcome of the war?

It is apparent from the Table of Figures (page 16) that the Central Powers were greatly outnumbered in forces, warships and population, even without taking French and British colonies into account. Allied numerical superiority was further increased by the remnants of the Belgian and Serbian armies; in addition Portugal and Romania joined the Allies in 1916 – though neither country was renowned for its military prowess. On the other hand, Bulgaria, the only further ally gained by the Central Powers after 1914, contributed a well-trained army half a million strong. Economically too the Allies were superior – and they had the extra advantage of loans and war supplies from the world's economic giant, the USA.

But bare statistics rarely tell the whole story. The outcome of the war was not determined simply by comparative amounts of men and military equipment. Less tangible factors would also help to decide the result. Austria's restive ethnic minorities, Turkey's discontented Arab population, Russia's militant Communists and Italy's poorly motivated conscripts all threatened to undermine their countries' war efforts. And any army fighting on the Western and Eastern Fronts might break under the strain of heavy casualties and appalling conditions. Morale (whether military or civilian) is not a commodity which can easily be measured by contemporaries or historians and it was not clear whose would be the first to collapse.

Obviously American participation after April 1917 added greatly to the resources and the morale of the Allies. The USA brought with it fresh troops, a sizable navy and a huge demographic, industrial and agricultural capacity, thus tipping the scales even further against the Central Powers (see page 110). President Wilson also brought with him his famous Fourteen Points, which stressed ideals such as democracy, self-determination and peace rather than national self-interest. Although these threatened to break the complex web of secret deals made by the Allies over the last two years, the advent of America did not in practice transform the war into an ideological struggle between liberalism and autocracy. For soldiers like A. A. Milne (who was serving as a Signals Officer on the Western Front) it was the 'Same old bloody war'.[11]

References

1 Figures from P. Kennedy, *The Rise and Fall of the Great Powers* (Fontana, 1989), pp. 255–61, Ferguson, *Pity of War*, p. 252 and G. Darby, 'The Great War' in *History Review* (September, 1998), p. 25.
2 R. Chickering, *Imperial Germany and the Great War* (CUP, 1998), p. 31.

3 E. Lussu, *Un anno sull'Altipiano* (Oscar Mondatori, 1970), p. 63. Translated by Carolyn Cooksey.
4 P. Haythornthwaite, *The World War One Source Book* (Arms and Armour Press, 1992), p. 302.
5 *Ibid.*, p. 301.
6 Channel 4 Documentary, *Mutiny*, 10 October 1999.
7 D. Stevenson, *The First World War and International Politics* (OUP, 1988), p. 137.
8 N. Stone, *The Eastern Front* (Hodder & Stoughton, 1975), p. 36.
9 Stevenson, *International Politics*, p. 119.
10 M. Clark, *Modern Italy, 1871–1982* (Longman, 1984), p. 187.
11 From 'Gold Braid' by A.A. Milne (the children's writer) in Gardner, *Up the Line to Death*, p. 129.

Answering structured questions on Chapter 2

a) To what extent did the Allies' initial resources surpass those of the Central Powers? (*10 marks*)
b) How did the aims of the two sides change after the beginning of the war? (*10 marks*)
c) Why did Germany's success depend on a short war and how did its aims and those of its enemies make this unlikely? (*20 marks*)

Structured questions like these are designed to lead you on from the presentation of relevant information in the earlier question(s) to valid conclusions in the final one.

Question a: Use the statistics on page 16 and the information given in the text for the countries participating in the war in 1914 (Germany, Austria and Turkey against Britain, France, Russia and Japan). It should be clear that the Allies' combined resources were greater than those of the Central Powers; the challenge is to decide how significant this superiority was. Remember to take into account countries' geographical position, as this could determine how their resources could be used.

Question b: Use the study diagram on pages 26–27 as well as the relevant text to find out how both sides formulated their aims after the war began and changed them as the fighting proceeded. The information presented in these answers should lead on to the conclusions demanded in Question c.

Question c: The inferior resources of Germany and the inadequacies of its allies provide explanations for the first part of the question. Its grandiose ambitions, the determination of their enemies to resist these and the Allies' own developing aims help to explain why neither side was willing to make an early peace.

Summary Diagram
The Belligerents' Aims and Resources

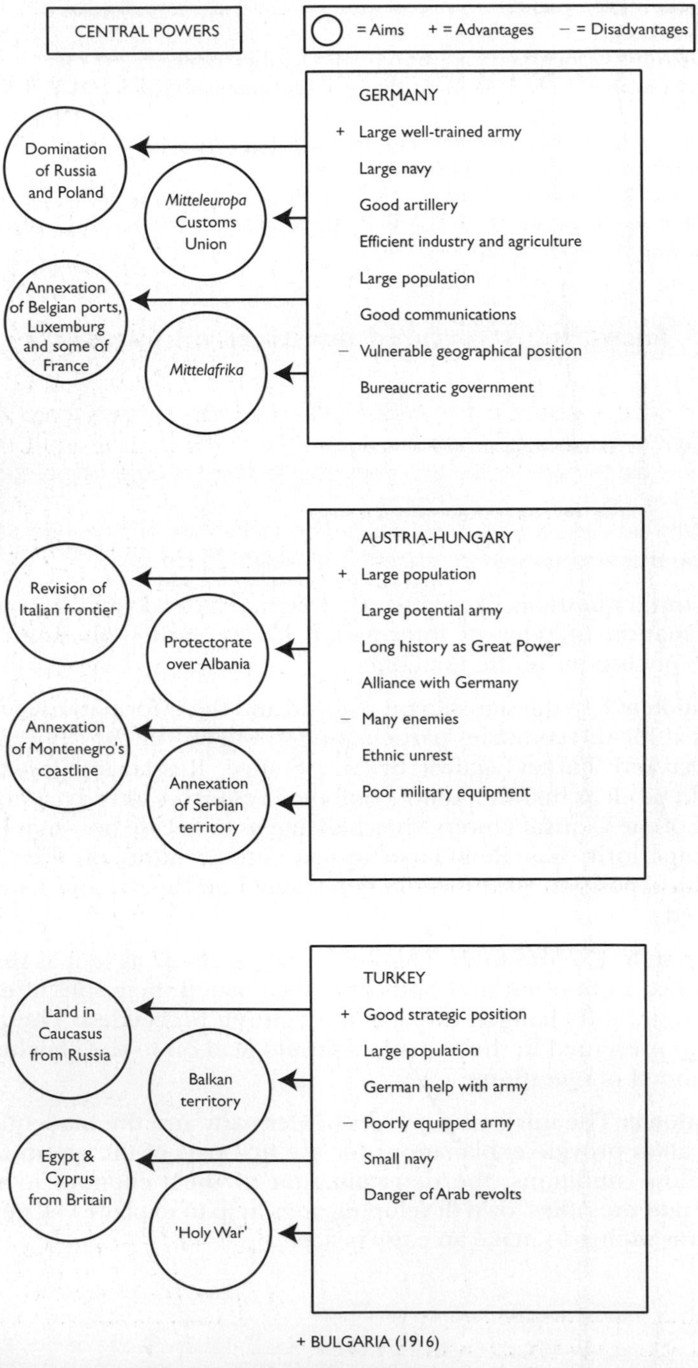

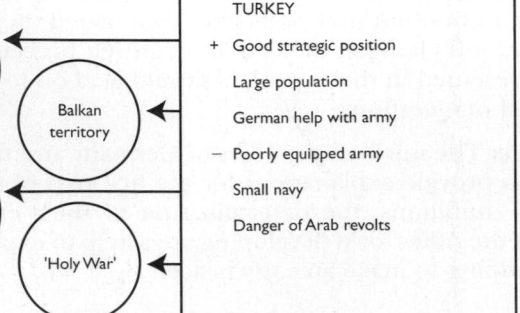

| CENTRAL POWERS | ◯ = Aims   + = Advantages   − = Disadvantages |

GERMANY

+ Large well-trained army

Large navy

Good artillery

Efficient industry and agriculture

Large population

Good communications

− Vulnerable geographical position

Bureaucratic government

Domination of Russia and Poland

Mitteleuropa Customs Union

Annexation of Belgian ports, Luxemburg and some of France

Mittelafrika

AUSTRIA-HUNGARY

+ Large population

Large potential army

Long history as Great Power

Alliance with Germany

− Many enemies

Ethnic unrest

Poor military equipment

Revision of Italian frontier

Protectorate over Albania

Annexation of Montenegro's coastline

Annexation of Serbian territory

TURKEY

+ Good strategic position

Large population

German help with army

− Poorly equipped army

Small navy

Danger of Arab revolts

Land in Caucasus from Russia

Balkan territory

Egypt & Cyprus from Britain

'Holy War'

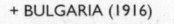

+ BULGARIA (1916)

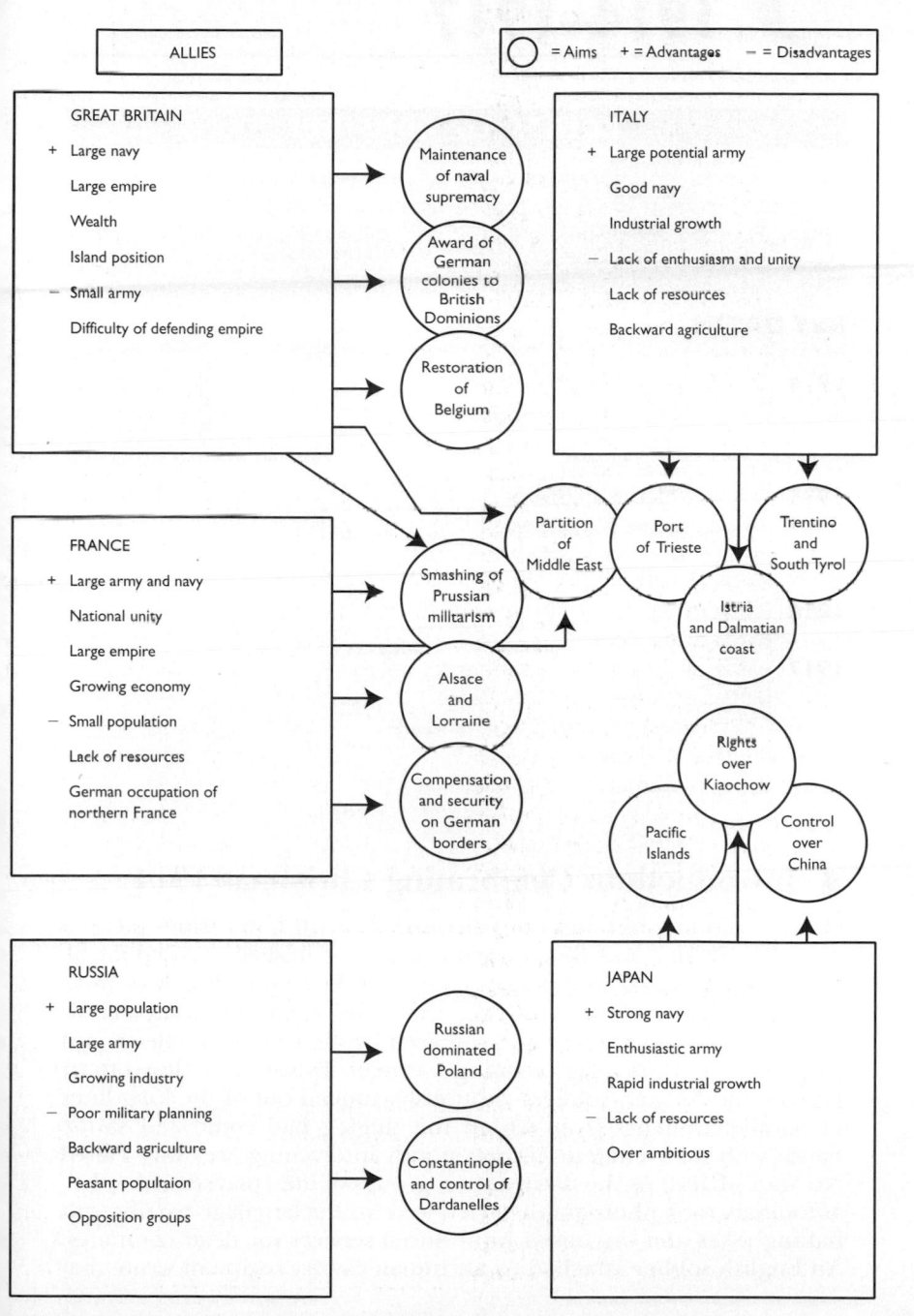

ALLIES

◯ = Aims   + = Advantages   − = Disadvantages

GREAT BRITAIN

+ Large navy

Large empire

Wealth

Island position

− Small army

Difficulty of defending empire

Maintenance of naval supremacy

Award of German colonies to British Dominions

Restoration of Belgium

ITALY

+ Large potential army

Good navy

Industrial growth

− Lack of enthusiasm and unity

Lack of resources

Backward agriculture

Partition of Middle East

Port of Trieste

Trentino and South Tyrol

Istria and Dalmatian coast

FRANCE

+ Large army and navy

National unity

Large empire

Growing economy

− Small population

Lack of resources

German occupation of northern France

Smashing of Prussian militarism

Alsace and Lorraine

Compensation and security on German borders

Rights over Kiaochow

Pacific Islands

Control over China

RUSSIA

+ Large population

Large army

Growing industry

− Poor military planning

Backward agriculture

Peasant population

Opposition groups

Russian dominated Poland

Constantinople and control of Dardanelles

JAPAN

+ Strong navy

Enthusiastic army

Rapid industrial growth

− Lack of resources

Over ambitious

+ BELGIUM and SERBIA (1914) + PORTUGAL (1916), ROMANIA (1916)

3 Stalemate on the Western Front 1914–1917

POINTS TO CONSIDER

After a brief description of how Christmas was celebrated on the Western Front in 1914, this chapter goes on to consider why the fighting in France and Belgium continued for so long after the date by which both sides had expected victory.

KEY DATES

1914 German advance into Belgium
Battles at Mons and Le Cateau
Battle of the Marne
First Battle of Ypres
1915 Battle of Neuve Chapelle
Second Battle of Ypres with first use of gas
Idea of tank proposed by Churchill
Battle of Loos
1916 Battle of Verdun
Battle of the Somme
1917 Battle of Champagne and French mutiny
Battles of Arras and Vimy Ridge
Third Battle of Ypres (Passchendaele)
'Mutiny' at Etaples
Battle of Cambrai

1 Introduction: Celebrating Christmas 1914

On the cold moonlit night of Christmas Eve 1914, in various parts of northern France and Belgium, the voices of unseen men could be heard singing carols in different languages. From one direction arose the strains of '*Stille Nacht*', from the other came 'O Come All Ye Faithful' or '*Minuit, Chrétiens*', followed by the sounds of cheers and laughter. On Christmas morning German, British and (less often) French and Belgian soldiers cautiously climbed out of the long lines of parallel trenches from which the singing had come and shook hands with their enemies in the muddy intervening area they called No-Man's Land. As the day went on groups of men played each other at football, took photographs, tried to cross the language barrier with halting jokes and organised joint burial services for dead comrades. An English soldier attached to an Indian cavalry regiment wrote that he would never forget the sight of 'our greatest enemy shaking hands with our Indian troops'. In some places this Christmas goodwill lasted into Boxing Day or longer; elsewhere the soldiers went back to exchanging bullets and shells rather than cigars and plum puddings.

When told of this unofficial, piecemeal truce, the British Commander-in-Chief, Sir John French, issued immediate orders to prevent any recurrence of such conduct and the German authorities also forbade any future fraternisation. 'My God', exclaimed one of the Germans who had shaken hands with the Indian soldiers, 'why cannot we have peace and let us all go home!'[1] It was a good question.

2 Gaining and Saving Territory 1914

> **KEY ISSUE** Why did Germany fail to knock France out of the war in 1914?

a) The German Invasion of Belgium

The German army of one and a half million which invaded Belgium on 3 August in accordance with the Schlieffen plan had certainly been confident of a quick victory. Nor did the French troops who marched eagerly into Alsace and Lorraine in their blue coats and red caps and trousers doubt that they would be successful in reclaiming their lost provinces. And the British Expeditionary Force of 160,000 men, which hastened to Belgium's rescue, did not expect to fail in that mission.

The Germans met with more Belgian resistance than they had anticipated. But they were able to crush this with the help of weapons like the enormous siege guns known as Big Berthas, which destroyed Belgium's fortresses, and with their policy of *Schrecklichkeit* (frightfulness). 'All who get in the way must take the consequences', General Moltke warned the Belgian people, whose plight now gave the Allies much material for useful propaganda.[2] (See also page 83.) By 20 August Brussels was under German occupation. The French rapidly transferred troops from Alsace and Lorraine where their attack had failed miserably. These, together with the BEF, held up the German advance at Mons and Le Cateau but suffered heavy casualties and were forced to retreat. Scenting victory as his army crossed the French frontier, Moltke made the mistake of diverting troops to fight the Russian invaders on the Eastern Front. This, combined with further losses inflicted by the French, meant that the Germans lacked the troops to encircle Paris as Schlieffen had planned and had to approach the city only from the east. These changes were to prove disastrous. They can be followed, as can the other battles mentioned in the chapter, on the Summary Map (page 51).

b) The Battle of the Marne

Meanwhile Paris emptied as residents fled and over two million reservists left for the front, using every possible means of transport, including 600 taxis. By 2 September the Germans had pushed British and French troops south of the River Marne, only 25 miles from Paris. They had marched over fifteen miles a day in intense heat; one British officer found it difficult to believe that his men could be 'so tired and so hungry and yet live'.[3] But the German army, which had been in continuous advance for 33 days, was even more exhausted and ill-supplied and was unable to resist combined British and French attacks along the Marne (6–12 September). Paris was saved by the Germans' decision to withdraw, though their troops were able to retreat in good enough order to dig themselves in on high ground north of the River Aisne, a position which they were able to hold against further attacks by the Allies. Moltke was now a 'broken man' and had to be replaced by General Falkenhayn.

c) The First Battle of Ypres

In October the Germans tried to outflank the Allies by launching an attack in the coastal plains of Belgian Flanders. Although outnumbered by two to one, British forces (which included vital Indian reinforcements) held the line in desperate fighting around the town of Ypres. By the time the battle ended in late November, 'when both sides accepted the onset of winter and their own exhaustion',[4] the BEF was almost wiped out. Yet even as savage a critic of the British High Command as Australian historian John Laffin has to admit that the only way to check the German advance was by this 'dogged resistance'.[5]

As Christmas approached both sides were entrenched on the Western Front. Germany, having conquered most of Belgium and a tenth of France, had to defend its position in the west as well as fighting on the Eastern Front. The Allies, having saved Paris and the French Channel ports, now faced the task of ousting the enemy. These manoeuvres had so far cost the Germans 667,000 casualties (i.e. killed and wounded), the French 995,000 and the British 96,000, a scale of loss unimaginable before the war. Germany and France could call up more conscripts and reservists. But Britain still relied on volunteers and Kitchener used his famous poster campaign to create a 'New Army' of three million men.

3 Establishing Stalemate

KEY ISSUE Why was it so difficult for either side to break through the enemy's trench system?

a) The Trench System

The trenches of the Western Front now extended for about 700 miles, from the Belgian Channel coast, through the flat marshlands of Flanders, across the river valleys of the Somme, the Oise and the Aisne in northern France, over the hilly, wooded areas of the north-east bordering on Alsace and Lorraine to the Swiss frontier. The distance between trenches varied but could be as little as 100–200 metres. There were significant salients (bulges) around Ypres and the ancient French fortress of Verdun, both of which were strategically important to the Allies. As time went on the trench systems became more complex. Rooms dug in their sides provided a little comfort and shelter – though Joffre discouraged French troops from making themselves at home lest they should lose the urgent will to attack; deeper bunkers (especially on the German side) afforded protection from heavy gunfire; communication trenches gave access for soldiers, supplies and stretchers to support and reserve trenches and to Casualty Stations. Most trenches were zigzagged to render them less open to enemy fire and all were protected at the front by parapets of sandbags and thick rolls of barbed wire. A diagram below from the notebook of Second Lieutenant Eric Heaton shows the ideal trench system. The photograph of Canadian troops at Passchendaele in 1917 suggests that reality did not always match this ideal (see page 32).

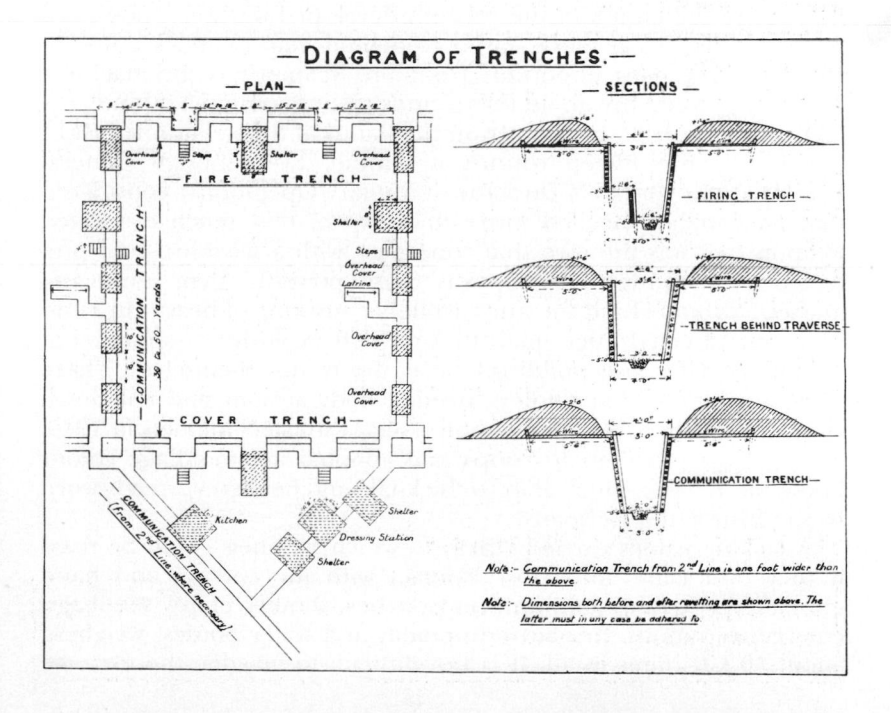

Compare this photograph of 'trenches' during the Battle of Passchendaele with the trench system visualised in an officer's notebook (previous page).

b) Weapons

Because of the nature of the recently-developed weaponry possessed by both sides, it was much easier to defend than to attack a line of trenches. The most important front-line weapon was the machine-gun, which could fire about 600 rounds of ammunition a minute – as compared to rifles which (even in the hands of the well-trained BEF) could only fire fifteen rounds a minute. Even though General Douglas Haig (Britain's Director of Military Operations) considered that no battalion needed more than two of this 'much over-rated weapon',[6] it was the case that 'one man with a machine gun, protected by mounds of earth, was more powerful than advancing masses.'[7] From behind the lines artillery consisting of heavy guns and howitzers directed huge quantities of high explosive or shrapnel at enemy trenches and buildings or at the troops themselves. There were suggestions that soldiers needed body armour and chainmail visors; in practice they were simply issued with steel helmets in 1915. By this time too French troops had adopted a camouflage colour known as 'horizon-blue', akin to the khaki and field-grey already worn by the British and Germans.

Attacking troops carried rifles (to which bayonets could be fixed if they ever came into close contact with the enemy) and hand grenades, as well as ammunition pouches, shovels, empty sandbags, emergency rations, first-aid equipment and water bottles, weighing about 30 kilograms in all. It is not difficult to imagine the extreme vulnerability of these men as they emerged from their trenches and advanced across No-Man's Land, where refuge was provided only by blasted trees and shell craters. Since telephone cables were likely to have been cut advancing troops could communicate with the rear only by using runners and flag signals. In most battles on the Western Front more troops were killed in the attack than in the defence.

c) A Typical Battle: Neuve Chapelle 1915

The Battle of Neuve Chapelle, fought in early spring 1915 by General Haig's First Army, illustrates the difficulty of gaining territory by offensive action, though this was considered by Haig to be the 'most soldierly way out of what looks like an impossible situation'.[8] On 10 March, after a heavy artillery barrage on the German trenches, British and Indian infantry divisions attacked along a front of several miles. It was planned that the cavalry would follow once the breakthrough had been made. At the centre of the attack the ruined village of Neuve Chapelle and four lines of German trenches were temporarily captured. In the northern sector, however, all the attacking troops (nearly 1,000) were killed as they tried to cross No-Man's land or cut the enemy wire. Haig (who was 40 miles behind the front line at his comfortable headquarters) insisted that the battle should continue 'regardless of loss'. By 13 March, after German counter-attacks, about 1,000 metres had been taken at the cost of about 12,000 casualties.

One of them was an Indian soldier who wrote in a letter home, 'This is not war. It is the ending of the world.'[9] A senior member of Haig's staff concluded that 'England will have to accustom herself to far greater losses than those of Neuve Chapelle before we finally crush the German army'.[10] He was right – future battles were to be far longer and more deadly. But, as General 'Bull' Allenby remarked when warned that there would be heavy losses at Ypres later that year, 'What the Hell does that matter? There are plenty more men in England!'[11]

4 Looking for Alternatives 1915

> **KEY ISSUE** Were there any alternative weapons or tactics which might have broken the deadlock on the Western Front?

a) New Weapons

It was Germany's new Chief of Staff, Falkenhayn, who first decided to use poison gas on the Western Front in an attempt to compensate for shifting more troops to the east. On 22 April 1915 German troops wearing respirators advanced towards Ypres behind a cloud of chlorine gas. Allied High Command had been alerted to impending gas attacks but had not issued any protection to troops, thousands of whom were incapacitated. Within a few days, however, British and Canadian soldiers were given linen masks with instructions to moisten them with their own urine. Armed with this simple device and with exceptional courage, the British held on to Ypres, but they suffered 70,000 casualties compared to half that number of Germans. Chlorine gas was a demoralising new weapon, which could cause death to unprotected victims; General Charteris, for instance, saw casualties of the 1915 battle 'slowly drowning with water in their lungs'. Phosgene gas, developed later, was more often lethal. Mustard gas, introduced in 1917, resulted in burning and blistering of the skin as well the temporary or permanent blindness memorably portrayed in the picture by the American war artist, John Singer Sargent (page 140).

Gas did not prove decisive, however, because both sides used it and in time issued effective respirators to their troops. The death rate among those affected was three per cent and the damage done was usually much less than that inflicted by shells and gunfire. Moreover, gas could endanger those using it if the wind changed direction (as it did for British troops at the Battle of Loos in September 1915) or if the storage equipment leaked. It continued to be used throughout the war as a disabling 'strategical' weapon.

An obvious way to avoid the paralysis of the Western Front battlefields was to take to the air. From 1914 Germany, France and Britain developed the use of aeroplanes for military reconnaissance, which proved most effective especially after the introduction of aerial photography. Inevitably air combat ensued, although at first this was a matter of taking potshots from the open cockpit with a revolver. In 1915 the Allies pioneered a forward-firing machine-gun which could be operated by pilots and a more sophisticated version of this was developed by the Germans. Both sides continued to improve their aircraft, which could increasingly be used for bombing enemy trenches and support lines. But, for all the skill and heroism of 'ace' pilots like the famous Baron von Richthofen, this form of warfare did not become a deciding factor before 1918, since neither side had a marked superiority.

War was also waged underground after British battalions began using miners to tunnel under No-Man's Land to the enemy's trenches, which could then be blown up with explosive charges. Mining and counter-mining became a permanent feature of the war and sometimes led to terrifying subterranean combat. Some of the resulting explosions, like that at Messines Ridge in 1917, could be heard and felt as far away as London. British miners (sappers) were probably the most proficient but they could not achieve a breakthrough.

A more novel idea was put in 1915 to the British Prime Minister, Asquith, by his First Lord of the Admiralty, Winston Churchill. 'Steam tractors with small armoured shelters' and a 'caterpillar system' could cross trenches and barbed-wire entanglements 'quite easily'.[12] The idea of the 'tank' (the deceptively innocent name given to this device) met with a mixed reception but work on it began in Britain under the direction of its inventor, Ernest Swinton. None were ready for use until 1916 and these few were clumsy and vulnerable. They were first put to effective use in the early stages of the battle of Cambrai in 1917 and in 1918 they played an important part in the last stages of the war. Opinions still differ on whether tanks were a war-winning weapon but the advantage in this field certainly lay with the Allies, since Germany was slow to take up the idea and produced only a few by 1918.

b) New Tactics

British High Command introduced no tactical innovations in 1915. Still hoping that the cavalry (in which most senior officers had been trained) would win the war, they insisted on maintaining large numbers of horses on the Western Front, using up much valuable shipping space for fodder. With their greater battle experience the French were developing new techniques of attack, such as having their troops advance in short bursts behind a 'creeping barrage' of artillery fire. Both the Allies continued to place their faith in offensive action. Germany, meanwhile, concentrated more on building up its defensive system with concrete machine-gun posts, deep ranks of artillery and sophisticated front-line shelters. A battle which demonstrated the effectiveness of these methods was fought in the autumn at Loos, where German fire mowed down thousands of attacking British troops – among them Rudyard Kipling's son (see pages 1–2). Some historians consider that Britain too should have adopted more imaginative and flexible methods of defence, using 'scattered strongpoints rather than continuous trenches'.[13]

Thus by the end of 1915 there seemed no realistic alternative to a long war of attrition; this meant trying to wear the enemy down by inflicting more casualties on them than they could cause in return.

5 Wearing Down the Enemy 1916

> **KEY ISSUE** Is it fair to accuse the generals' strategy of attrition of causing 'useless slaughter' on the Western Front?

a) The Battle of Verdun

General Falkenhayn's decision to launch an offensive on the French fortress system around Verdun is a perfect example of planned attrition. He predicted that French pride would not allow them to give up this old garrison town without a struggle and made the gruesome calculation that three French soldiers would die for every German killed. Thus France would be 'bled white'.

He was right in his first assumption. After being surprised by the fierce attack (one of the first to use flamethrowers) on 21 February and having to surrender Fort Douaumont four days later, Joffre put the Verdun sector under the command of General Pétain, who was renowned for his defensive tactics. 'They shall not pass', Pétain declared and this became the watchword of France. Between February and July French troops and supplies were poured into Verdun and the battle became a hell from which neither side could escape. By June the Germans had taken another stronghold north of Verdun, Fort Vaux, and they came within a few miles of the Verdun fortress, beneath which thousands of French soldiers were housed. The whole area had become a morass of mud and rubble by July, when Germany abandoned the attack and replaced Falkenhayn with Generals Hindenburg and Ludendorff. In the autumn the French counter-attacked and recaptured both the captured forts, whose grim underground caverns are still displayed to the public. The final toll of this battle has been variously estimated; it probably amounted to half a million French and more than 400,000 German casualties. In the bloody arithmetic of attrition the Germans had miscalculated. They launched no further offensives on the Western Front until 1918.

b) The Battle of the Somme

Before this battle ended another had begun. Since March 1916 the Allies had been planning a joint attack in the Somme area. Kitchener's 'New Army' of volunteers had arrived on the Western Front and Haig (who had now replaced French as Commander-in-Chief) was anxious to make British strength felt. He still hoped for a breakthrough though Joffre's aim was simply attrition. Because of the mounting pressure on Verdun the date for the start of the battle was brought forward to 1 July and it was agreed that the British would play the greater part.

For a week before that date the Germans were bombarded with a heavier barrage of artillery than had ever been used before: about one and a half million shells were fired. This was supposed to destroy their wire, trenches, guns and communications and to make it impossible for them to emerge from their dugouts. After that the troops were to advance in four successive rows along an 18-mile front, at the walking pace which was thought most suitable for inexperienced troops, occupy the enemy trenches which would be unmanned and break through to their reserve lines. The cavalry would then be able to follow up. In practice the artillery bombardment, which consisted of more shrapnel than high explosive, was extremely unpleasant and unnerving for the Germans, who had to spend days in their nine-metre deep shelters, but it did not destroy all their wire, let alone their trenches and gun emplacements. It did, however, make enormous craters in No-Man's Land and cut all the British telephone cables. Haig's second-in-command, General Rawlinson, knew that the artillery had not done its job and thought it better 'to proceed by shorter steps'. He did not communicate this to his chief, who disliked any criticism of his plans. Haig's confidence was undented; he wrote in his diary on 30 June that the men were 'in splendid spirits', and that the wire had 'never been so well cut, nor the artillery preparation so thorough'.

The artillery bombardment stopped shortly before the attack was due to start at 7.30 in the morning of 1 July – giving the Germans just enough time to race to their parapets and man their machine-guns. As the attackers went over the top, fortified if they were lucky by generous issues of strong rum, they were mown down. Some battalions were entirely destroyed within minutes, though a few succeeded in reaching the enemy lines and gaining their objectives. It was the worst day in British military history with 60,000 casualties, of whom 20,000 had been killed. Haig wrote on 2 July that the casualty figures (which he was told were 40,000) could not 'be considered severe in view of the numbers engaged, and the length of front attacked'.[14]

Committed as he was to his plan, Haig allowed the battle to continue for four and a half months, involving troops from Australia, New Zealand, Canada, Newfoundland and South Africa as well as Britain and France. In the later stages tanks were used for the first time; they terrified the Germans but there were too few of them to make a real impact. The cavalry was never deployed. By the time it ended during abominable weather in November about 650,000 Allied soldiers had been killed or wounded, compared to around 500,000 Germans. More precise figures cannot be given but it is clear that more fell in the attack than in the defence. One survivor describes the sense of personal loss as 'almost unbearable.'

Had this human tragedy achieved anything in military terms? About six miles of territory were gained – four miles short of the first day's objectives. Obviously there had been no significant breakthrough. The clearest Allied gain was the relief of Verdun, as early on in the battle Falkenhayn had had to move several battalions from there to the Somme. In addition, according to military historian Gary Sheffield, this battle had turned the British army into a 'hard-bitten and effective' force.[15] It is also true that German as well as Allied soldiers had been pushed to the limits of human endurance. Some historians consider that the combined losses of Verdun and the Somme contributed significantly to the ultimate defeat of Germany, though such long-term effects are difficult to quantify.

Another result of this battle was probably a greater tendency for soldiers to question the war and the way it was being waged, though this would only be done in private or not admitted until later. A few days before his death a German soldier expressed 'the hope that it may be possible to find some way out of this miserable situation'.[16] In the 1970s a British soldier told the First World War historian, Lyn MacDonald that 'it was criminal to send men in broad daylight, into machine-gun fire, without any cover of any sort whatsoever'.[17]

6 Experiencing the Trenches

> **KEY ISSUE** How did the troops manage to endure the horrors of fighting in the trenches?

a) The Mud and the Stars

It was not only during battle that soldiers faced the danger of death or wounds. In the front line and in the reserve trenches they might at any moment be shot by a sniper, gassed or blown to pieces by a shell, mine or bomb. At night, patrols would be sent out into No-Man's Land to recover dead and wounded comrades, carry out repairs, spy on the enemy, take prisoners or cut the wire if an attack was planned; few such parties returned intact. The troops also fell prey to dysentery and 'trench fever' as a result of filthy conditions and exposure. They suffered from typhoid caused by the lice which bred in their clothes and they were liable to get a fungal infection known as 'trench foot' in the frequently wet, muddy conditions. They had to share their dugouts and their food with disease-ridden rats fattened on a plentiful supply of rotting corpses. In addition, venereal disease affected many soldiers even in the British army, which had been exhorted by Kitchener to 'avoid any intimacy with women'.

The combination of boredom, lack of sleep, deafening gunfire, loss of friends, gruesome sights and constant danger drove many men to psychological collapse – a condition which in time came to be diagnosed and treated as 'shell-shock'. Many soldiers longed for a relatively minor wound or illness which would allow them to escape from the trenches. Some inflicted injuries on themselves, an offence for which they could, if convicted by a court martial, be shot by firing squad. Recently opened files reveal that 3,080 death sentences were passed on British soldiers, though nine tenths of these were commuted to hard labour. The other armies on the Western Front executed proportionately fewer; the French about 700 and the Germans only 48.

But most of the young men serving in the German, French and British armies found ways of 'soldiering on'. The cheerful companionship of their 'pals', looking forward to leave, simple diversions like concerts, film shows and football matches, the inspiring leadership of many junior officers, patriotism and a resilient optimism all helped to keep up troops' morale for much of the time. Many found solace in religion, especially on the eve of a battle, while most relied heavily on their issues of rum to give them 'Dutch courage and a lurching contempt for danger'.[18] Decent food supplies were so important that in one battalion the men voted that two military medals due to them after a successful attack should be awarded to the cooks. Tobacco companies provided free cigarettes for the troops, nearly all of whom smoked heavily. Some soldiers actually found the war exciting, describing it afterwards as the greatest adventure of their lives. There is also evidence that in all armies a 'live and let live' mentality made life a little more tolerable; in some areas, for instance, there were unofficial truces during breakfast or after heavy rain.

As one young officer wrote, it was possible in the trenches to see 'both the mud and the stars'.[19]

b) Soldiers' Testimony

Evidence of the physical experiences and complex emotions of soldiers in the different armies comes from a variety of sources. (It can be quoted in essay questions like the one on page 68.)

Siegfried Sassoon, a British writer, pays tribute in his war diary to the men in his battalion:

1 *March 30 1916*
  Their temper is proven, the fibre of their worth is tested and revealed; these men from Welsh farms and Midland cities, from factory, shop and mine, who can ever give them their meed of praise for the patience and
5 tender jollity which seldom forsake them? The cheerless monotony of their hourly insecurity, a monotony broken only by the ever-present imminence of death and wounds – the cruelty and malice of these things that fall from the skies searching for men, that may batter and pierce the bodies and blot the slender human existence.[20]

In the same year the French Socialist writer, Henri Barbusse, used his own trench diaries as the basis for a novel *Le Feu*. It was immediately published in Paris and translated into English as *Under Fire* in 1917, despite its realistic portrayal of the war. In this passage the soldiers in his battalion discuss why they 'stick it':

1 Says Corporal Bertrand, 'There's only one thing you need to know, and it's this; that the Boches are here in front of us, deep dug in, and we've got to see that they don't get through, and we've got to put 'em out, one day or another – as soon as possible.'
5 'Yes, yes, they've got to leg it, and no mistake about it. What else is there? Not worth while to worry your head thinking about anything

else. But it's a long job.' An explosion of profane assent comes from
Fouillade, and he adds, 'That's what it is!'
'I've given up grousing,' says Barque. 'At the beginning of it, I played hell
10 with everybody – with people at the rear, with the civilians, with the
natives, with the shirkers. Yes, I played hell; but that was at the beginning of the war – I was young. Now, I take things better.'
'There's only one way of taking 'em – as they come!'
'Of course! Otherwise you'd go crazy. We're dotty enough already, eh,
15 Firman?' ...
Silence follows the recorded opinions that proceed from these dried
and tanned faces, inlaid with dust. This, evidently, is the credo of the
men who, a year and a half ago, left all the corners of the land to mass
themselves on the frontier: Give up trying to understand, and give up
20 trying to be yourself. Hope that you will not die, and fight for life as well
as you can.[21]

In 1916 the eighteen-year-old Erich Maria Remarque had just grad-
uated from high school and arrived in the German trenches. His
experiences there gave rise to the vivid writing which made his novel
All Quiet on the Western Front a best-seller when it was published in
1929. In this passage his hero's depleted battalion enjoys a rest
period:

1 Thus for the moment we have the two things a soldier needs for con-
tentment: good food and rest. That's not much when one comes to
think of it. A couple of years ago we would have despised ourselves ter-
ribly. But now we are quite happy. It is all a matter of habit – even the
5 front line. Habit is the explanation of why we seem to forget things so
quickly. Yesterday we were under fire, today we act the fool and go
foraging through the countryside, tomorrow we go up to the trenches
again. We forget nothing really. ... But our comrades are dead, we
cannot help them, they have their rest – and who knows what is wait-
10 ing for us? We will make ourselves comfortable and sleep, and eat as
much as we can stuff into our bellies, and drink and smoke so that the
hours are not wasted. Life is short.[22]

Many participants recalled their war experiences in memoirs and
autobiographies. In an unpublished memoir Philip Heath looks back
on the relationship he had as an eighteen-year-old subaltern with the
Thames bargemen under his command:

1 I had never met anyone before like the men in my Company. They were
a fairly rough crew. I liked them for their cheerfulness and for the general kindness with which they treated me, for they often went out of
their way to show me the ropes and make life easier for me. In return
5 I became a sort of unofficial scribe for many of them who were almost
illiterate.[23]

One of the most famous autobiographies covering the war period is *Goodbye To All That*, written in 1929 by Sassoon's friend and fellow-writer, Robert Graves. Here he remembers night patrols:

1 At dusk [during the battle of Loos in 1915], we all went out to get in
   the wounded, leaving only sentries in the line. . . . We spent all that night
   getting in the wounded of the Royal Welch, the Middlesex, and those
   Argyll and Sutherland Highlanders who had attacked from the front
5 trench. The Germans behaved generously. I do not remember hearing
   a shot fired that night, though we kept on until it was nearly dawn and
   we could see plainly; then they fired a few warning shots, and we gave
   it up. . . . Every night we went out to fetch in the dead of the other battalions. The Germans continued indulgent and we had few casualties.
10 After the first day or so the corpses swelled and stank. I vomited more
   than once while superintending the carrying.[24]

Many First World War veterans have recorded their memories in tape-recorded interviews. Ulick Burke describes conditions in the British trenches during the battle of Passchendaele:

1 Now you can imagine a man being in those trenches for a week, where
   he couldn't wash. He got a petrol tin of tea given him. Now those tins
   were baked, boiled, everything was done to them; but when you put a
   hot substance in you got petrol oozing from the tin. And that of course
5 gave the men violent diarrhoea. But they had to drink it because it was
   the only hot drink they had. The conditions were terrible. You can
   imagine the agony of a fellow standing for twenty four hours sometimes
   to his waist in mud, trying with a couple of bully beef tins to get water
   out of a shell hole that had been converted to a trench with a few sand-
10 bags. And he had to stay there all day and night for about six days. That
   was his existence. Many men got trench feet and trench fever. With
   trench fever a fellow had a very high temperature, you could see he
   had. It wasn't dysentery but he had constant diarrhoea, it left him weak
   and listless. Trench feet was owing to the wet sogging through your
15 boots. In many cases your toes nearly rotted off in your boots. We lost
   more that way than we did from wounds.[25]

Contemporary medical records are also of great use to the historian. Here a German staff surgeon reports cases of shell-shock at Fort Douaumont near Verdun in 1916:

1 Nervous disorders could be observed in great quantity. Shock, confusion, loss of speech, hysteria, cramps, delirium, and other various psy-
   choses, among which I especially noted amentia [imbecility]. The
   horrible scenes of mass carnage in the dark passageways of the fort, the
5 picture of horribly decimated corpses, combined with the moaning of
   the wounded, the death-rattling sounds of the dying, the screaming and
   ranting of the mad – all this heightened the horrors after the catas-
   trophe to the edge of human resistance.[26]

Millions of letters were sent to their loved ones by soldiers in all the trenches. Censored though they were they provide an invaluable record. In this letter written four days before his death in the battle of Passchendaele (26 October 1917), Jack Mudd tells his wife of the companionship which has consoled him through terrible times:

1 Out here dear we're all pals, what one hasn't got the other has, we try to share each other's troubles, get each other out of danger. You wouldn't believe the Humanity between men out here. Poor little Shorty, one of the fellows that came out with me, he used to tell me all
5 about his young lady, his Hilda, ... and when he got home he would get married and come over to see me and introduce her to you. He used to make me laugh with his talk, how he loved his Hilda but unfortunately he will never see her again poor fellow .... I often think of him yet poor fellow I don't think he has a grave but lies somewhere in the open. Still
10 dear I don't want to make you sad but it just shows you how we seem to stick together in trouble. It's a lovely thing is friendship out here. Please God it won't be long before this war is over, we are pushing old Fritz back, I don't think he will stand the British boys much longer and then we will try and keep a nice home. I will know the value of one
15 now.[27]

A German chronicle suggests that Private Mudd's impression of a demoralized enemy was not entirely correct. In *Storm of Steel*, published very soon after the war, Ernst Junger conveys the thrill of battle he experienced at Cambrai in 1917:

1 Cracks of thunder showed us our way. Behind rifles and machine-guns hundreds of eyes lay in wait upon the goal. We were already far in front of our own lines. From all sides shots whistled round our steel helmets or shattered with a harsh clap on the trench's rim. ... Then we hurled
5 ourselves forward. Scarcely had a look glanced over the crumpled body of a foe who had played out his hand than a new duel began. The hand-grenade exchange reminds you of foil fencing; you have to spring as in a ballet. It's the deadliest of contests for two, and it's ended only when one of the opponents goes flying into the air.[28]

Probably more common in all armies was the longing for peace expressed in soldiers' songs, like this sardonic verse sung to the tune of the hymn 'What a Friend we Have in Jesus':

1 When this lousy war is over,
  No more soldiering for me,
  When I get my civvy clothes on,
  Oh, how happy I shall be!
5 No more church parades on Sunday,
  No more putting in for leave,
  I shall kiss the sergeant-major,
  How I'll miss him, how he'll grieve![29]

Another source of humour was the trench newspapers like

Bystander, in which Bruce Bairnsfather's cartoons made jokes about the harsh conditions endured by his many fans in the British army. The caption to the example given (reproduced as a collectable picture postcard) draws attention to an instruction in the Military Manual:

'Every encouragement should be given for singing and whistling'.[30]

The sign in the cartoon refers mockingly to an *estaminet* – a soldiers' café like those described in the short story *The Square Egg,* written in the trenches by H.H. Munro (Saki) not long before his death in the battle of the Somme.

ı When one is thinking about mud one is probably thinking about *esta-minets.* ... An *estaminet* is a sort of compound between a wine-shop and a coffee-house, having a tiny bar in one corner, a few long tables and

benches, a prominent cooking stove, generally a small grocery store
5 tucked away in the back premises, and always two or three children
running and bumping about at inconvenient angles to one's feet. ...
Perhaps there is nothing in the foregoing description to suggest that a
village wine-shop, frequently a shell-nibbled building in a shell-gnawed
street, is a paradise to dream about, but when one has lived in a drip-
10 ping wilderness of unrelieved mud and sodden sandbags for any length
of time one's mind dwells on the plain-furnished parlour with its hot
coffee and *vin ordinaire* as something warm and snug and comforting in
a wet and slushy world.[31]

No doubt, too, the *estaminets* were frequented by women willing to
provide the soldiers with some comfort, though the subject of sex was
rarely mentioned at the time, even in French soldiers' news sheets. A
brief glimpse of their longings appears in *Le Midi au Front*:

1 Those girls from the mining villages were attractive to look at. Tall and
slim, with dark eyes. They offered us hospitality: a table in a corner,
chairs, a lamp for the evenings. ... And then a little love here and there,
a snatched kiss, a brief embrace, sometimes more. You went off to the
5 trenches and you thought about them, at night, in the dugout, under the
shelling.[32]

Saki also wrote an essay about an unexpected source of joy experienced by many soldiers in the trenches – *Birds on the Western Front*.
Dauntless skylarks, singing 'a song of ecstatic jubilation' often
cheered soldiers in the 'chill misty hour of gloom that precedes a
rainy dawn'.[33] Such a moment is also captured by Isaac Rosenberg, a
Jewish poet and painter from the East End of London who served in
the British trenches from 1915 until he was killed in 1918:

1 Sombre the night is:
And though we have our lives, we know
What sinister threat lurks there.
Dragging these anguished limbs, we only know
5 This poison-blasted track opens on our camp –
On a little safe sleep.

But hark! Joy – joy – strange joy.
Lo! Heights of night ringing with unseen larks:
Music showering on our upturned listening faces.

10 Death could drop from the dark
As easily as song –
But song only dropped,
Like a blind man's dreams on the sand
By dangerous tides;
15 Like a girl's dark hair, for she dreams no ruin lies there,
Or her kisses where a serpent hides.[34]

7 Floundering in the Mud 1917

> **KEY ISSUE** Why and at what cost did the stalemate continue to the end of 1917?

1917 saw a continuing struggle on the Western Front. As a result of their losses on the Somme the Germans shortened their line of trenches, withdrawing 25 miles in the central part of the front to a highly-mechanised defensive network six to eight miles in depth – the 'Hindenburg Line'. On the Allied side there were changes at the top. In Britain David Lloyd George, the dynamic Minister of Munitions, had taken over as Prime Minister from Asquith in 1916. In France General Nivelle took the place of Joffre as Commander-in-Chief. Haig remained in command of the British army.

The early months of the year were a critical time for the Allies. Russia was in the throes of revolution and the USA had not yet entered the war. Even after the Americans' declaration of war in April it would be many months before their troops were ready to serve on the Western Front.

a) French mutinies

Soon after taking up his post Nivelle assured his own army and the British Prime Minister that the Allies would soon be 'at Berlin'. To this end he launched a great April offensive in the Champagne area. Despite improved tactics, great heroism and enormous casualties, only front-line trenches were taken, German defensive positions proving too strong. The high hopes aroused by Nivelle, combined with miserable conditions, led in May to mutiny in the French army. Thousands of *poilus* simply left the trenches and refused to obey their officers' orders to go back into the line. For about two weeks there was chaos in the French sector until Nivelle was sacked and the new Chief, Pétain, quelled the mutiny by responding to the men's complaints while at the same time imposing strict military discipline. 629 men were sentenced to death (though only 43 were actually shot) and immediate improvements were made in the pay, leave and diet of French troops. Haig disapproved of these concessions and said that 'Pétain ought to have shot 2,000'. In any case, the mutiny was over and effectively hushed up but it was clear that the French army was in no fit state for immediate further attacks. Pétain declared that he was waiting for the Americans and tanks.

b) The Battle of Passchendaele

There had as yet been no mutiny among British troops on the Western Front though the Battles of Vimy Ridge and Arras (April 1917) had been severely testing. The Canadian troops who gained the crest at Vimy in a sensational victory were prevented by 'the usual inflexibility of the plan' from progressing to the German-held coal mines and railways on the plain beyond.[35]

There had been an individual act of protest by Sassoon who, after being wounded at Arras, issued a public statement on 15 June to the effect that the war was 'being deliberately prolonged by those who have the power to end it'. For this 'wilful defiance of military authority' he could have been court-martialled; instead he was diagnosed as suffering from shell-shock and sent to Craiglockhart War Hospital. He and other 'half-dotty' officers, including the poet Wilfred Owen, received humane psychological treatment here from Dr W.H.R. Rivers. Sassoon was judged sane enough to be 'discharged for duty' in December.

Meanwhile General Haig showed no reluctance to compensate for the French army's 'weariness and disappointment' as reported to him by Pétain.

1 12 June.
It is my considered opinion, based not on mere optimism but on a thorough study of the situation, guided by experience which I may claim to be considerable, that ... the British armies are capable and can be relied
5 on to effect great results this summer – results which will make final victory more assured and which may even bring it within reach this year. ... Given sufficient force, provided no great transfer of German troops is made in time from east to west, it is probable that the Belgian coast could be cleared this summer, and that the defeats on the
10 German troops entailed in doing so might quite possibly lead to their collapse.

Lloyd George was loath to agree to this plan for a new battle in the Ypres salient, preferring to send divisions to Italy or the Near East, but in June he gave the go-ahead for a short campaign.

By the time the attack began on 31 July a preliminary bombardment of over four million shells, together with the heaviest rain for decades, had turned the whole area into a swamp. Nevertheless, Haig was pleased with the first day's action:

1 31 July
This was a fine day's work. General Gough thinks he has taken over 5,000 prisoners and 60 guns or more. The ground is thick with dead Germans, killed mostly by our artillery. I sent Alan Fletcher and Colonel
5 Ryan round the Casualty Clearing Stations. They report many slight cases, mostly shell fire. Wounded are very cheerful indeed. ... I told Gough to carry out the original plan.[36]

The weather remained wet for most of the battle which, despite Lloyd George's intentions, continued until 6 November; long before this the mud had become so deep and liquid that men and horses drowned in it while vehicles and guns sank without trace (see picture on page 32). A sergeant serving in a Field Ambulance Division recorded these conditions in his diary:

1   14 August
    The casualties suffered holding the line have been something terrible.
    The infantry took a few pill-boxes and a line or two of trenches from
    the enemy in this attack but at a fearful cost. It is only murder attempt-
5   ing to advance against these pill-boxes over such ground. Any number
    of men fall down wounded and are either smothered in the mud or
    drowned in the holes of water before succour can reach them.[37]

Gruelling advances against German counter-attacks (which involved the first use of mustard gas and air bombardment of troops) resulted eventually in Canadian divisions capturing Passchendaele ridge and the village of that name, which had virtually disappeared. Haig's last report on the battle reads:

1   6 November
    The operations were completely successful. Passchendaele was taken.
    ... The whole position had been most methodically fortified – yet our
    troops succeeded in capturing all their objectives early in the day with
5   small loss – 'under 700 men'. ... Today was a very important success.[38]

The Ypres salient had been deepened by five miles – but the Belgian coast was still far away. The Allies lost about 320,000 men in this effort; as with other battles, German casualty figures are hard to determine but they were probably in the region of 200,000.

It is perhaps a symptom of the lowered morale resulting from this battle that in September 1917 British soldiers protested violently against the rigours of military training at the Etaples camp. Mutiny was averted by speedy concessions and one corporal was executed as an example to others.

c) The Battle of Cambrai

On 23 November 1917 the British public thought that victory had come when church bells rang all over the country; they were signalling a significant breakthrough at Cambrai where 324 tanks had been used to drive the Germans five miles back in one day. But many of the tanks broke down subsequently and, as a result of Passchendaele, there were insufficient troops to engage the German reinforcements who were quickly sent to Cambrai. Once again the cavalry were denied their chance to gallop through the lines. In the end, nothing was gained at Cambrai; tanks were still not a war-winning weapon.

d) A Useless Slaughter?

There can be no denying that the battles of 1915, 1916 and 1917 killed, disfigured, blinded, dismembered or deranged thousands of young men; even Haig's respectful biographer, John Terraine, describes the period of attrition as a 'holocaust'.[39] What historians still disagree about is whether the slaughter caused by British offensives in particular served any useful purpose.

Terraine and other supporters of Haig argue that the Germans could not simply be left to sit on the defensive and that the French army would have collapsed without heavy British engagement. Since there was no wonder-weapon which could achieve victory there was no alternative but to wear the enemy down. Heavy casualties, according to Gary Sheffield, were inevitable. A recent article by an American historian concludes that Haig deserves credit for his 'dogged determination' and that he contributed much to the war's outcome.[40] Terraine accepts Haig's own verdict that the cause of victory in 1918 lay 'in the great battles of 1916 and 1917'.[41]

Critics insist that Haig was a cold, aloof figure with, Keegan considers, 'no concern for human suffering'.[42] He did not adapt quickly enough to modern methods of warfare and continued to value the cavalry and the bayonet more highly than the machine-gun or the automatic rifle. Thus he was slow to adopt tactics which integrated artillery with infantry in such a way as to save lives. Instead he stuck for too long to the unimaginative and costly method of massive attacks along a broad front. He is accused, in Laffin's words, of 'criminal negligence'.[43] Gerard de Groot judges him more fairly as 'a creature of his society'; he was 'the best commander available' but, he adds, 'this reveals as much about the Army as a whole as about Haig'.[44]

e) Peace or War?

1917 had seen calls for peace coming from widely differing quarters. President Wilson of America had tried to arrange mediation; the new Emperor Karl of Austria-Hungary had attempted to negotiate a settlement with France; the German Reichstag (Parliament) had passed a peace resolution; Pope Benedict XV, the British Conservative politician Lord Lansdowne and the Russian Communist leader Lenin had all published appeals for an end to the fighting. But no governments were prepared to make the concessions necessary for a negotiated peace. The new French Prime Minister, Georges Clemenceau, was determined to lead his country to victory. He told the Chamber of Deputies that it would be 'War, nothing but War!' Lloyd George declared that there was 'no halfway house between victory and defeat'.[45] In Germany Hindenburg and Ludendorff, who were confident of victory now that Russia had been defeated, did not find it difficult to overrule the Reichstag.

So the fourth Christmas of the war brought no peace to the Western Front. On 28 December Private Eccles wrote to his mother telling her of how he had spent the festive season as part of a bombing party on the icebound Passchendaele Ridge. They were spotted by the Germans who opened up an artillery barrage:

1 It was the worst half hour I have ever spent. Casualties were heavy and
   many were the cries of wounded men. In one place no less that four
   men had their heads blown off. . . . I may be wrong in telling you all this,
   but the reason I do is that it is some record of exciting adventure which
5 I never dreamed of. But here I am, I am not worrying so you need not.
   I am in the pink, barring being a bit stiff and bruised. But believe me anything is preferable to that Hell upon earth, Passchendaele Ridge. . . . The
   weather is severe, but we get hardened. We are having our Christmas
   feed on Sunday, a big pay day. I have plenty of fags, and a fine pipe so I
10 am très bon. Meanwhile we are nearer the end of the war. . . . May next
   Christmas be quieter for me.[46]

Chapter 6 will examine the 'adventures' which Eccles and his fellow soldiers had to go through before Christmas 1918.

References

1 Both quotations are from A.J. Peacock (ed), *Gun Fire* (Western Front Association), Vol. 1 No. 2 , p. 66.
2 J. Winter & B. Baggett, *The Great War* (Penguin Books, 1996), p. 65.
3 M. Gilbert, *First World War* (Weidenfeld & Nicolson, 1994), p. 67.
4 J. Keegan, *The First World War* (Hutchinson, 1998), p. 142.
5 J. Laffin, *British Butchers and Bunglers of World War One* (Alan Sutton, 1988), p. 30.
6 Gilbert, *First World War*, p. 199.
7 A.J.P. Taylor, *The First World War* (Hamish Hamilton, 1963), p. 29.
8 Laffin, *Butchers and Bunglers*, p. 12.
9 D. Omissi, *The Sepoy and the Raj* (Macmillan, 1994), p. 114.
10 Gilbert, *First World War*, p. 133.
11 L. James, *Imperial Warrior: The Life and Times of Field-Marshal Viscount Allenby* (Weidenfeld & Nicolson, 1993), p. 75.
12 Quoted in Gilbert, *First World War*, p. 124.
13 Laffin, *Butchers and Bunglers*, p. 172.
14 This quotation and the previous one are from R. Blake (ed), *Private Papers of Douglas Haig* (Eyre & Spottiswoode, 1952), pp. 151 & 154.
15 BBC, Timewatch, *Douglas Haig:The Unknown Soldier* (1998).
16 P. Witkop (ed), *German Students' War Letters*, trans. A.F. Wedd (Methuen, 1929), pp. 229–30.
17 Quoted in L. Macdonald, *Voices and Images of the Great War* (Penguin Books, 1988), p. 160.
18 J.E. Lewis (ed), *True First World War Stories* (Robinson, 1997), p. 225.
19 M. Brown, *The Imperial War Museum Book of the Western Front* (BCA, 1993), p. 265.
20 S. Sassoon, *Diaries 1915–1918*, ed. R. Hart-Davis (Faber & Faber, 1983), p. 48.
21 H. Barbusse, *Under Fire* (Everyman's Library, 1969), pp. 26–7.
22 E.M. Remarque, *All Quiet on the Western Front*, trans. A.W. Wheen (Putnam's, 1929), pp. 154–5.

23 P.G. Heath, *Forty Years After*, unpublished MS at the Imperial War Museum, p. 8.
24 R. Graves, *Goodbye To All That* (Penguin Books, 1960), pp. 133–4 & 137.
25 M. Brown, *The Imperial War Museum Book of the First World War* (Sidgwick & Jackson, 1991), p. 55.
26 Quoted in Herwig, *The First World War*, p. 298.
27 Brown, *The First World War*, p. 71.
28 T. Nevin, 'Ernst Junger: Storm Trooper and Chronicler' in H. Cecil and P. Liddle, *Facing Armageddon* (Leo Cooper, 1996), pp. 271–2
29 Used in the musical by Joan Littlewood, *Oh What a Lovely War*.
30 Imperial War Museum Picture Archive.
31 Saki, *The Complete Saki* (Penguin, 1982), pp. 540–1.
32 S. Audoin-Rouzeau, *Men at War* (Berg, 1992) p. 130.
33 *The Complete Saki*, p. 547.
34 I. Rosenberg, 'Returning, We Hear the Larks' in Gardner, *Up the Line to Death*, p. 104.
35 Keegan, *First World War*, p. 352.
36 Last three quotations from Blake, *Private Papers*, pp. 246, 238 and 250.
37 Brown, *Western Front*, p. 188.
38 Blake, *Private Papers*, p. 264.
39 J. Terraine, *Douglas Haig* (Hutchinson, 1963), p. 481.
40 F. Vandiver, 'Haig and Pershing' in Cecil & Liddle, *Armageddon*, p. 76.
41 Terraine, *Douglas Haig*, p. 482.
42 Keegan, *First World War*, p. 311.
43 BBC, Timewatch: *The Unknown Soldier*.
44 G. de Groot, *Douglas Haig* (Unwin Hyman, 1988), p. 6.
45 Gilbert, *First World War*, p. 389.
46 Macdonald, *Voices and Images of the Great War*, pp. 259–60.

Source-based questions on Chapter 3

a) Study the extract from Haig's diary, 12 June (page 46). How useful is this source for understanding Haig's reasons for launching this battle? (*6 marks*)

b) Study the extract from Haig's diary, 31 July, the sergeant's diary, 14 August (pages 46 and 47) and the picture on page 32. Describe and account for the differences and similarities in these depictions of conditions during the battle. (*10 marks*)

c) Use all these sources and your own knowledge to explain how far you agree with John Keegan's view that 'the point of Passchendaele defies description' and that it tipped the British army 'into the slough of despond'. (*15 marks*)

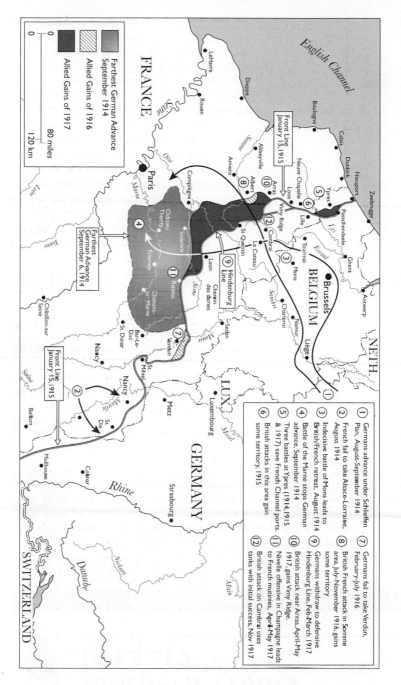

Summary Map The Western Front: 1914–1917.

Farthest German Advance September 1914
Allied Gains of 1916
Allied Gains of 1917

0
80 miles
0
120 km

1. Germans advance under Schlieffen Plan, August–September 1914
2. French fail to take Alsace-Lorraine, August 1914
3. Indecisive battle of Mons leads to British/French retreat, August 1914
4. Battle of the Marne stops German advance, September 1914
5. Three battles at Ypres (1914,1915 & 1917) save French Channel ports.
6. British attacks in this area gain some territory, 1915
7. Germans fail to take Verdun, February–July 1916
8. British/French attack in Somme area, July–November 1916, gains some territory
9. Germans withdraw to defensive Hindenburg Line, Feb–March 1917
10. British attack near Arras, April–May 1917, gains Vimy Ridge.
11. Nivelle offensive in Champagne leads to French mutinies, April–May 1917
12. British attack on Cambrai uses tanks with initial success, Nov 1917

4 The Eastern and Southern Fronts 1914–17

POINTS TO CONSIDER

This chapter moves from the Western Front to other areas of land fighting: eastern Europe, the Middle East and Italy. The summary map on page 00 as well as the text should help to explain how the various fronts affected each other. The important question for students, as for war leaders at the time, is whether any of the other fronts was as crucial as the Western Front. It is also interesting to compare the experiences of soldiers in these widely differing theatres of war.

KEY DATES

1914 Austrian campaign against Serbia begins
Defeat of Russia in East Prussia
Turkey's Caucasus campaign begins

1915 Gallipoli campaign against Turkey begins
Bulgaria's entry into the war
Armenian massacres begin
Italy's entry into the war
Four Battles of the Isonzo
Defeat of Russia in Galicia
Defeat of Serbia
Chantilly Conference of Allies

1916 Allied evacuation of Gallipoli completed
Five Battles of the Isonzo
British surrender at Kut
Austrian offensive in the Dolomites
Brusilov offensive against Austria begins
Romania's entry into the war

1917 March Revolution in Russia
Entry of Greece into the war
Allenby's campaign in Palestine begins
Lawrence of Arabia's guerrilla campaign
November Revolution in Russia
Austrian breakthrough at Caporetto
British capture of Jerusalem
Russian armistice
Romanian cease-fire

1 Introduction

While Belgians fled from villages burned by the Kaiser's advancing forces in August 1914, Germans themselves were made homeless by two Russian armies invading the area of their country known as East Prussia. The sight of refugees bringing pramloads of possessions and barefoot children into Berlin presented the German government with a dilemma: should it concentrate all its efforts on defeating France or should it jeopardise the Schlieffen Plan by sending troops to halt the Russian invasion?

Such difficult choices confounded all the major belligerents over the next three years. Austria-Hungary dithered disastrously between dealing with Serbia and Italy to the south and contending against Russia to the north-east; Russia had to send out armies against Germany, Austria and Turkey; Britain and France were torn between the Western Front's need for more men and supplies and appeals for relief from their hard-pressed ally. When various Balkan countries entered the war, still more fronts were opened up and harassed wartime leaders struggled to keep abreast of the different areas of fighting.

2 Halting the 'Steam-roller': The Russian Fronts

> **KEY ISSUE** What factors led to the defeat and eventual collapse of Russia?

a) Battles in East Prussia and Galicia 1914–15

On 19 August 1914 General Prittwitz, the German Commander in East Prussia, made a frantic telephone call to Berlin. He warned that he could not resist the First and Second Russian Armies moving to the north and south of the Masurian lakes and that he would have to retreat. It was only when the German Commander-in-Chief sent Generals Hindenburg and Ludendorff to take over his command that the outnumbered German forces were able to outmanoeuvre an enemy which was utterly unprepared for modern warfare. Undetected by incompetent Russian intelligence, Ludendorff surrounded General Samsonov's Second Army to the south of the lakes and soundly defeated it near the village of Tannenberg on 27–30 August. 90,000 bewildered Russian soldiers gave themselves up and further tens of thousands retreated in disarray over the Russian border. German soldiers searching the forests for booty (guns, horses and equipment which filled 60 trains) found the body of General Samsonov, who had shot himself in the head rather than face the Tsar after such a humiliating defeat.

With communications in complete disorder, the First Russian Army, 50 miles away to the north of the lakes, had been unable to prevent this disaster. It held out until early September, when two extra divisions sent over from the Western Front gave the Germans superiority. Between 7 and 13 September, in the Battle of the Masurian Lakes, Hindenburg pushed the Russians back over the frontier and by the end of the year he had gained a secure hold over East Prussia. This campaign had cost over 100,000 German casualties. The Russian army had also suffered huge losses. The fact that it had contributed to the failure of the Schlieffen Plan was probably not much comfort to its peasant soldiers, many of whom lacked overcoats, boots and adequate rations.

Further south, in the Polish-speaking borderlands of Austria-Hungary and Russia, an even more confused conflict was taking place. Austria's Chief of Staff, Count Conrad von Hötzendorff, sent troops into Galicia in August, with no clear idea of what they were meant to achieve. Encountering superior numbers of Russian soldiers, they were defeated in battles in the region of Lemberg. By October Austria had given up 150 miles of territory and 100,000 prisoners. Further retreat was only prevented by the arrival of German troops under General Falkenhayn. Over the winter 'men froze and starved amid the steep valleys and forests' of the Carpathian mountains.[1] Keegan applies this description only to the Austrians but in fact it is difficult to say which army suffered more.

Fighting resumed in January 1915 with a joint German-Austrian offensive in January aimed at the final defeat of Russia. The Russians counter-attacked but when German reinforcements arrived in the spring the overloaded Russian transport system could not bring up sufficient reserves to match them. By this time, too, the Russian shell-shortage was so acute that guns were limited to ten shots a day. Florence Farmborough, an English nurse serving on the Russian front, recorded in her diary: 'Whole regiments are said to be without a cartridge and only a certain number of batteries can continue the shelling.'[2] In May and June Russia was defeated in the extended Battle of Gorlice and forced to retreat from Galicia. German troops also invaded Russian Poland and took Warsaw on 5 August – 'a breathtaking spectacle'.[3]

Historians such as Norman Stone and Orlando Figes draw attention to the poor state of the Russian army at this stage. Written evidence is sparse because so many soldiers were illiterate and letters were strictly censored. The readiness with which men surrendered to the enemy, long sick-lists and the frequency of self-inflicted injury attest, however, to the 'widespread demoralisation of the army'.[4] Figes identifies the occasion of this retreat as a 'vital psychological moment' and quotes from the diary of Dmitry Os'kin, a literate peasant who had become a platoon commander:

> What are we doing in this war? Several hundred men have already passed through my platoon alone and at least half of them have ended up on the fields of battle either killed or wounded. What will they get at the end of the war?[5]

Nevertheless, in spite of losing 75,000 casualties and retreating 250 miles, Russia was able to fight on once its armies had been reorganised and re-equipped. Britain and France were at that time trying to relieve the pressure on their ally by taking on Turkey in Gallipoli (see pages 57–60). It is also worth noting that these campaigns had severely damaged the Austrian army, which could no longer manage without German help. Its rates of desertion and surrender were proportionately higher than Russia's because of the disloyalty of non-German-speaking troops, who resented their cruel treatment and poor rations.

When Tsar Nicholas II unwisely assumed supreme command of the Russian army in August 1915 the outcome of the war in eastern Europe still hung in the balance. Diplomatic efforts by the Central Powers to conclude a separate peace with Russia in the course of the year met with no response.

b) The Brusilov Offensive 1916

At a conference held at Chantilly in France in December 1915 Britain, France, Italy and Russia decided to co-ordinate their strategy: all four countries were to make simultaneous attacks on the Central Powers. Russia's role was to launch first a major offensive against Germany and then a minor one against Austria. Such plans proved easier to make than to carry out.

It is true that a gigantic industrial effort had resulted in thousand-fold increases in Russia's production of war materials between August 1914 and early 1916. There was no longer a shell-shortage, though commanding officers continued to use it as an excuse for failure or inaction. Since Russia still had the largest army in Europe, in spite of difficulties with conscription, there seemed no reason for its not carrying out the promise made at Chantilly. Once Germany had begun its onslaught on Verdun in February the French urged quick action. The result was an ill-planned offensive on Russia's north-west front during the March thaw of 1916; waves of Russian infantry were mown down by German artillery for no gain at all. Most Russian officers (many of whom were elderly) had now lost the will to attack.

One who was still determined to prove Russia's worth as an ally was General Brusilov. An intelligent commander who made tireless efforts to improve the conditions of his men, he is considered by most historians to be Russia's most successful First World War leader. Despite having fewer men and supplies than his colleagues in the north-west, he was keen to press ahead with an attack on Austria-Hungary. After carefully concealed preparations and with unprecedented co-ordination between artillery and infantry, he carried this out all along the

Galician front in June. By August he had won one of the greatest victories of the war, regaining much of the territory lost in 1915 and dealing an irreparable blow to the Austrian army. Figes believes that this battle could have changed the course of the war had it not been for 'military stupidity'.[6] Considering it a side-show, the government sent no reserves to make up for the million casualties it had cost. Thus all Brusilov's gains had to be relinquished in the face of counterattacks organised by Hindenburg later in the year.

Nevertheless, the offensive had profound effects. It helped to save Verdun by causing German reinforcements to be diverted from the Western Front; it contributed to Romania's decision to enter the war on the side of the Allies; and it brought the Austrian army close to collapse. Brusilov became a hero in Europe, although his reputation in Russia seemed less secure. He recorded that he regularly received anonymous letters from his own soldiers warning 'that they did not want any more fighting, and that if peace was not concluded shortly, I should be killed.'[7]

c) The Collapse of Russia 1917

The despair expressed by Russian soldiers sounds similar to that which caused mutiny in the French army in 1917. Troops of both nations anguished about bad conditions and irregular leave, expressed concern for the plight of their families and longed for peace. Why is it that the Russian army collapsed in July 1917 while the French was pacified by Pétain's concessions?

The crucial factor was the state of the Russian economy. The industrial boom generated by the war solved the shell-shortage but in doing so it created massive inflation. The most serious effect of this was that peasants hoarded their grain rather than selling it for devalued money. The inadequate supplies released were sporadically distributed by a transport system which could not cope with the demands of the war. Soldiers waiting for their rations at the front or in barracks were as easy a prey for revolutionary propaganda as civilians queueing for bread in the cities; the government's ban on vodka sales inflamed passions still further. When the people of Petrograd (as St. Petersburg had been named) rose against the Tsar in March 1917 the Petrograd garrison refused to defend him and he quickly fell from power.

The Provisional Government which now took control decided to continue with the war and appointed Brusilov as Commander-in-Chief. But not all soldiers were enthusiastic about a renewed war effort even under more popular leadership. Many were more influenced by the Petrograd Soviet (workers' council), whose famous 'Order Number One' gave soldiers the rights of citizens when they were not on military duty, established soviets in the ranks, introduced democratic forms of address and declared that troops should carry out government orders only if they did not conflict with those of the

Soviet. Brusilov blamed this 'accursed' document for destroying the discipline of the army.[8] Florence Farmborough was surprised to find that 'soldiers can now sit – even smoke – in the presence of their officers'.[9]

Nevertheless, Brusilov at first supported the decision taken by Alexander Kerensky, the new Minister of War, to launch a summer offensive. But when 'Mr General' (as Brusilov had now to be called) visited the front lines he found the troops disaffected and hostile to the idea of a new attack. 'If we take a mountain, there is always another one in front of us, and there is no profit in it', one soldier grumbled. In spite of Brusilov's doubts, the offensive took place on 1 July but it foundered after a couple of weeks. An English observer remembers that many men 'hid in the woods and only returned when they were sure that the fighting was over'.[10] Few battalions were as loyal as the 'battalion of death' made up of women led by Maria Botchkareva. Russian troops now retreated in a headlong rush from the front lines, denuding the countryside of anything which might provide sustenance for the German and Austro-Hungarian forces who pursued them far beyond the frontier. Russia's combatant role was now over, after 'three years of merciless, senseless slaughter'. It is hard to disagree with the Bolshevik writer, Maxim Gorky, who attributes the cruelty often shown by his fellow-revolutionaries to the brutalizing effects of 'this bloody nightmare'.[11]

No official armistice was made until December, after Lenin's Bolshevik party had seized power. At the opening of formal peace negotiations in Brest-Litovsk on 22 December the chief German delegate thought it auspicious that they were beginning 'in sight of that festival which for many centuries has promised peace on earth and good will towards men'.[12] More heartfelt was the Germans' hope that after Christmas they would be able to send most of their troops to fight on the Western Front.

3 Dealing with the 'Minor Powers': Turkey and the Balkans

> **KEY ISSUE** Why did fighting in the Balkans and Turkey continue for so long?

a) The Gallipoli Campaign 1915

'Let me bring my lads face to face with Turks in the open field', wrote General Sir Ian Hamilton, Commander of Britain's army in Gallipoli. 'We must beat them every time because British volunteer soldiers are superior individuals to Anatolians, Syrians and Arabs and are animated with a superior idea.'[13] This attitude is typical of the arrogance with which the 'Great Powers' assumed that they could easily defeat weaker or smaller countries. In fact Turkey and the Balkan nations often presented unexpected obstacles both to the Allies and to the Central Powers.

In spite of its serious recruitment problems and a woefully inadequate communications system, Turkey created major difficulties for the Allies after it entered the war in October 1914. By blockading the Dardanelles Straits Turkey prevented British and French help from reaching Russia; by threatening British trade interests around the Persian Gulf and the Suez Canal it forced Britain to keep garrisons in Mesopotamia (Iraq) and Egypt; and by attacking Russia in the Caucasus Mountains it drew Russian troops away from Eastern Europe. As it happened, Turkey's foolhardy winter campaign in the Caucasus resulted in a decisive Russian victory. This setback seems to have prompted the Ottoman government's horrifying genocide of its Armenian subjects, whom they suspected of being disloyal and a potential help to the enemy. Between April 1915 and December 1917 Armenians in towns like Trebizond were massacred and thousands more were marched into the desert where they died of starvation and thirst. Nearly 700,000 men, women and children disappeared in the first 'ethnic cleansing' of the twentieth century.

Meanwhile the Allies had embarked in 1915 on a venture which proved to be as ill-judged as Turkey's Caucasus campaign. Anxious to respond to Russia's appeals for help, desperate to find an alternative to the Western Front stalemate and hoping to attract new allies in the Balkans, the British War Council hesitantly adopted the idea of a Dardanelles offensive championed by the First Lord of the Admiralty, Winston Churchill. Even though the Navy would spare only some of its older vessels (apart from the 'super-Dreadnought' *Queen Elizabeth*), Churchill was confident that Constantinople could be taken 'by ships alone'. After bombardment of Turkish shore defences, 16 British and French battleships advanced into the Dardanelles on 18 March. At the end of the day, during which three ships had been sunk and a further three put out of action by undetected Turkish mines, the fleet commander, Admiral de Robeck, abandoned the operation. For weeks Churchill urged the renewal of the naval plan but instead he was blamed for its failure and forced to leave the Admiralty.

A plan was now improvised to land troops on Turkey's Gallipoli peninsula, to the north of the Straits. War Secretary Lord Kitchener, who did not consider the Turks a serious enemy, would allow only one division to leave the Western Front; apart from that, the 30,000 Australians and New Zealanders currently training in Egypt would be 'quite good enough'.[14] Hasty and inadequate though the preparations were, they were not complete until 25 April. By this time the Turks were ready too. On the morning of that day, after bombardment from the sea, various landing parties struggled to shore: a French diversionary force at Kum Kale on the Asiatic coast, British regiments on the beaches at the tip of the peninsula (Cape Helles) and the Anzacs (as the Australian and New Zealand troops were nick-named) ten miles away at Gaba Tepe – or 'Anzac Bay'. The Turks were greatly outnumbered but because they held the steep slopes and cliffs above the beaches they could slaughter the enemy as they landed. 'All day long', wrote an Australian Captain, 'we were losing cobbers [mates] and stretcher bearers were kept busy.' By the end of that day at least 4,000 out of the 30,000 who landed had fallen. Over the ensuing months troops fought to gain more than a foothold but Turkish counter-attacks prevented them from penetrating further than a few miles. In August, after reinforcements had arrived, a new landing was made at Suvla Bay further north. But General Stopford, 'an officer of advanced years and vacillating disposition',[15] failed to press forward when the Turks were initially taken by surprise; here too a deadly stalemate resulted.

By this time the Turkish forces had also been augmented and the two sides were evenly matched. Furthermore, the Turks were ably led by the German General Liman von Sanders and by a gifted young Ottoman commander, Mustapha Kemal, who inspired his men to fight courageously even when they lacked ammunition. British, French and Anzac soldiers also behaved with great heroism – but the leadership given by General Hamilton, who directed the campaign from his ship, was less dynamic than Kemal's. As well as the mis-judgements made by Hamilton and his subordinates, the troops had to endure an unbearably hot summer and an acute shortage of water supplies, the combination of which caused thousands to die of dysentery. For Private Ernest Lye the campaign was 'a terrible nightmare that I shall remember as long as I live'. Many of his fellow-soldiers must have felt the same but here, as on the Western Front, humour and comradeship kept men going. An Australian soldier explains how they carried on:

> In the Diggers we just trusted each other blind and while one bloke stayed there he could bet his sweet life that the other mate was going to be with him and that if we went we'd all go together.

Eventually, in October, Hamilton was relieved of his command; his successor, Sir Charles Monro, recommended the evacuation of the peninsula 'on purely military grounds, in consequence of the grave daily wastage of officers and men'.[16] The War Council did not finally decide on withdrawal until early December, by which time a ferocious blizzard had caused hundreds of soldiers to freeze to death or drown in floods. Churchill had already resigned from the government in protest against his colleagues' lack of commitment to the campaign. Between 30 December and 8 January all surviving troops and their equipment were evacuated; they left behind the remains of those who had died – 28,000 British, 10,000 French, 7,500 Australians and 2,250 New Zealanders. It is true that about 55,000 of the best Turkish troops had also perished, but at least the Turks could claim victory over the European invader.

Mustapha Kemal, who later became leader of Turkey, dedicated the peninsula as a memorial park. It is much visited by Australians, who remember this campaign with a mixture of pride and bitterness. It was not an episode of which the British government could be proud. Although some historians argue that the campaign came close to success, it is difficult to see how anything but a much greater commitment of planning, men and resources could have defeated Turkey at this time and place. Here was not an enemy which could be knocked out in a side-show.

b) The Balkans

One aim of the Gallipoli campaign had been to give support to Serbia, which was still unconquered. Three Austro-Hungarian armies had invaded on 12 August 1914, confident that they would 'force the Serbs to recognize Austria-Hungary's mastery'. The Serbs were outnumbered and at first taken off guard but General Putnik rushed reinforcements forward and soon pushed the invaders back over the borders. In September Austrian forces invaded a second time, although they had to be bullied into battle. Belgrade fell but the Serbs, now receiving supplies from the west, counter-attacked, regained their capital and freed the country of Austrian troops by the end of the year. In the process, however, 100,000 Serb soldiers were killed and a typhus epidemic subsequently claimed many more lives.

In 1915 Germany decided to assist in the conquest of this recalcitrant country, which blocked its communications with Turkey. The German government was also negotiating for an alliance with Bulgaria, designed to encircle Serbia. Once the Gallipoli campaign had begun to falter, in September, Bulgaria threw in its lot with the Central Powers, on condition that it would receive Macedonia (southern Serbia) as well as some Turkish territory. In October 600,000 German, Austrian and Bulgarian troops overran Serbia. The remnant of its army and thousands of civilian refugees retreated across the Albanian mountains, where they were beset by hostile local tribes. Enemy aeroplanes, severe winter weather, hunger and disease made their plight worse. The soldiers reached safety on the island of Corfu where they awaited the opportunity to free their country. 'For sheer heroism and endurance the Serbian retreat has few equals', concludes one historian.[17]

Bulgarian forces now established a strong position in the mountains of Macedonia. Among the Allied troops who were landed in the northern Greek province of Salonika to dislodge them was Private N.C. Powell, who describes the dangers of fighting in this land of 'untamed' beauty: 'Johnny Bulgar treated us to many displays of accurate shooting with trench mortars, grenades, machine guns and a few personal visits; these, coupled with malaria, played havoc amongst us.'[18] Bulgaria kept the Allies busy on the Salonika front until October 1918.

The third Balkan country to enter the fray was Romania. During the successful Brusilov offensive of August 1916 it was enticed to join the Allies with promises of Austrian land. It was soon attacked, however, by its hostile neighbours; by December German, Austrian and Bulgarian forces had overrun most of the country, including its oilfields and grain reserves which now helped to supplement Germany's dwindling resources. Russian troops diverted from Galicia had been unable to prevent this disaster. Romanian counter-attacks in 1917 achieved some success but Russia's collapse left Romania isolated and a cease-fire was arranged at the end of the year.

By this time Greece had at last joined the Allies. For three years Greeks had been split between the German-educated King Constantine, who wanted to keep his country neutral, and the liberal politician, Eleutherios Venizelos, who favoured intervention. The King had been unable to prevent the Allies from using Salonika as a base for their campaign against Bulgaria. Eventually, with Anglo-French support, Venizelos formed a government and forced the King into exile. He committed Greece to the Allies in June 1917 but brought them no immediate advantage as mobilisation was not complete until April 1918. At the end of 1917 the Central Powers were still dominant in South-Eastern Europe.

c) The Desert War

After the Allies withdrew from Gallipoli the Turks transferred troops to their Arab province of Mesopotamia. They had been holding British and Indian forces under siege at Kut since December 1915 and had overcome all attempts to relieve the city. By April 1916 the besieged were reduced to eating horses or taking opium pills to reduce hunger. At the end of the month they surrendered to the Turks, who took them on a forced march to prisoner-of-war camps in Anatolia. During this 'saga of pain and death' 2,500 Indian and 1,250 British troops died.[19]

The combined effects of defeat, bad climatic conditions, exhaustion and inadequate supplies lowered morale among Allied troops remaining in Mesopotamia. This was especially true in the Indian regiments where desertion and malingering were common. 'They are not fighting with much keenness and are rather homesick', concluded one army report.[20] The Chief Medical Officer blamed their malaise on deficient rations which led to a high rate of scurvy. Indian troops' provisions were only about a quarter of those of British soldiers and were particularly lacking in fresh meat and vegetables. With an improved diet (including 250 gallons a day of fresh lime juice shipped from India), their health and fighting efficiency began to improve in 1917. In February of that year the British recaptured Kut and then advanced to take Baghdad in March. They had gained ascendancy over the Turks in Mesopotamia, but had needed 200,000 men to do it.

Lest the Turks should try to retake Baghdad, the British government sent General Allenby to fight them in Palestine. It was also thought that a victory in the Holy Land would boost Allied morale. In addition Anglo-French imperialist ambitions would reap rewards in the Middle East as outlined in the Sykes-Picot Plan (see page 20). The force which Allenby had at his disposal in June 1917 consisted of experienced British and Anzac cavalry and infantry divisions with good air support. He also had guerrilla assistance from the anti-Turkish Arab Movement organised by Captain T.E. Lawrence (known as Lawrence of Arabia) and Sharif Hussain of Mecca, who had been given vague British assurances of Arab independence. In November, however, this accord with the Arabs was jeopardized by the Balfour Declaration, giving British support to the idea that Palestine would become a 'national home' for the Jews.

Allenby 'had learnt much since leaving France', according to his biographer.[21] Before launching his bid for Jerusalem in September, he looked after his troops' welfare by ensuring adequate water supplies and medical facilities. Even so, for the likes of Sapper H.P. Bonser the campaign involved a 'nightmare of interminable marching, thirst and tiredness'.[22] Conditions were even worse in Turkey's Palestinian army, which was also inferior in numbers and equipment. These advantages enabled Allenby's force to push its way north from Gaza and to capture Jerusalem in December.

When Christmas Day services were held in Jerusalem and Bethlehem, Bonser and his pals, who were busy laying cables in the desert, had a festive dinner consisting of 'two biscuits, a tin of bully beef to four and a tin of jam to seventeen men'. On Boxing Day the Turks (now with German reinforcements) made a bid to recapture Jerusalem; they were repulsed but they had shown that Turkey was still an enemy to be taken seriously.

4 Fighting in the Clouds: The Italian Front

KEY ISSUE How useful was Italy's contribution to the Allied war effort?

a) The Isonzo 1915–16

Italy's decision to declare war on Austria in May 1915 was inspired partly by confidence in the Allied cause at the beginning of the Gallipoli campaign. At this point Austria was heavily committed in

Serbia and Galicia and could not afford to send more than a few divisions to defend its south-western borders. But, like the Turks on the cliffs of Gallipoli, the Austrians occupied an advantageous position – the crests of the highest mountains of Europe, the Dolomites and the Alps. Against this natural fortress were pitted Italian conscripts, who were largely peasants from the south or city lads quite unused to mountain warfare. Their Commander-in-Chief, General Luigi Cadorna, was sure, nevertheless, that he could force his way through to Austria by driving his soldiers into constant attacks.

He chose as his first battleground Italy's north-east frontier, where the Austrians occupied the high plateau of Carso above the Isonzo river valley. Italian objectives included the Adriatic port of Trieste and its hinterland. On the Isonzo front Italian troops went on the offensive four times between May and November 1915, losing progressively more men each time and gaining no territory. In March 1916 attacks were resumed and by dint of five more battles during that year Italy gained the town of Gorizia and a foothold on the Carso. In this 'howling wilderness of stones sharp as knives'[23] both sides suffered high casualties caused by splintering rock. When Sergeant Benito Mussolini was wounded here 44 fragments were removed from his body; after his recovery he devoted himself to his newspaper, *Popolo d'Italia*, which was later to become a Fascist organ, repeatedly urging Italian soldiers to 'face the enemy'.[24] Another junior officer, Emilio Lussu, summed up the stalemate on the Isonzo in May 1916: 'We have done nothing but capture trenches, trenches and trenches – but the situation remained the same.'[25] A jingle sung by the troops suggested that if Cadorna wanted to see Trieste he should buy a picture postcard.

b) The Dolomites 1915–16

Another Italian objective was the Austrian Tyrol, even though most of its inhabitants spoke (and still speak) either German or a local language called Ladin. The high frontier in the Dolomite Mountains was very lightly defended in 1915 and the Italians were able to cross it in May; in fact the Austrians regarded it as a military miracle that they did not advance further. The ski resort of Cortina d'Ampezzo was taken by Italian soldiers who were 'disappointed with the coolness with which they were welcomed' by local people. For them, as for so many other civilians in disputed border areas, 'World War One was a disaster'.[26]

Austrian resistance stiffened after an order from General Conrad that troops 'should construct positions, place obstacles in front of them, and remain there'.[27] In July they repulsed 15 Italian attacks and here, too, stalemate ensued as the adversaries fought for possession of the high peaks. 'Clouds hang over us; clouds breathe our breath', wrote Captain Paolo Monelli of the skilled Italian *Alpini* troops, who

Contrast the battle conditions of Italian and Austrian troops in the
Dolomites with those on the Western Front.

often felt 'cut off from the world'. They had only one means of communication and supply – mules who 'go on unheeding amid shell-fire
and blizzard and find the path in night and fog'. Soldiers made 'warm
dens dug out of the rock, caves of darkness and stench' to protect
themselves both from enemy shell-fire and from temperatures which
fell to minus 30 degrees Centigrade at night.[28] Unknown to high command, men in opposing trenches, who had often been acquainted
with each other before the war, sometimes played cards or exchanged
coffee for *grappa* (brandy). In the Ampezzo region Italian soldiers
took messages to the families of their counterparts in the Austrian
army who could not go home on leave to villages under Italian occupation.

There was no such amity at the top, however. Conrad hated Italians
and in May 1916 launched a massive *Strafexpedition* (punishment

attack) in the Dolomites. After a bombardment which Lussu likened to 'an earthquake shaking the mountain', Austrian troops captured many peaks and passes. The Italians, who had been ordered to 'cling to the ground with tooth and nail', managed to limit the enemy advance to twelve miles. Later in the year they regained a third of this territory.

c) Austrian Breakthrough: Caporetto 1917

The Italian soldiers who had taken part in these battles were not well rewarded for their efforts. Pay was so low, rations so meagre and leave so infrequent that the men in Lussu's brigade concluded that 'those bandits prefer to have us starving hungry, thirsty and depressed. ... That way, it's all the same to us whether we live or die.'[29] There were no troop entertainments and soldiers were forbidden to enter cinemas and bars even when they were on leave. The only generous provision was of *grappa*, issued before battles and referred to as the *benzina* (motor-fuel) which kept soldiers going. They were also driven by 'a regime of unremitting harshness', enforced by officers who imitated Cadorna in their methods.[30] First-hand accounts tell of frequent summary executions at the front line. Sometimes an order came from 'those men down there, nicely shaved, with clean sheets'[31] that a decimation should be carried out: one in ten men were to be shot in regiments suspected of being mutinous. Firing parties often refused to carry out these orders. Lussu tells of an incident when shots were fired over the heads of the condemned men and then aimed at the major who had given the order. Another punishment took the form of soldiers being tied to trees in No-Man's Land where they would be exposed to crossfire.

It is not surprising that by October 1917, after further fruitless attacks on both fronts in the spring and summer, the Italian army was at a low ebb. It was then that the Austrians (now reinforced with German troops) launched a 'hurricane offensive' at Caporetto on the Isonzo. Assaulted by poison gas (against which they had no adequate protection), high explosive and formidable regiments like Rommel's *Alpenkorps*, Italian soldiers streamed down from the mountains. In 11 days they were pushed back 80 miles, as far as the River Piave, within striking distance of Venice. In the Dolomites too incursions were made and Cortina d'Ampezzo now welcomed the Austrians back. With only 10,000 killed, about 275,000 Italians had surrendered to the enemy and thousands more had deserted. To try to stop this rout Cadorna ordered the summary execution of all 'stragglers', an episode vividly evoked in Ernest Hemingway's *A Farewell to Arms*. His hero (loosely based on Hemingway himself, who served as an ambulance driver with the Italian army) has become separated from his regiment and escapes from the *carabinieri* (police) by jumping into the fast-flowing River Tagliamento.

Cadorna blamed the disaster of Caporetto on a pervasive social indiscipline and defeatism which caused 'a kind of military strike' in the army. Historians attribute it rather to Cadorna's own mistakes; he had created conditions which facilitated enemy success in the Isonzo valley and he made inadequate preparations once he suspected an attack was coming. Clearly discipline often did break down at this point but there is no evidence of a soldiers' strike. No orders were given and 'troops simply retreated as fast as they could'.[32]

Anyway, Orlando's new government dismissed Cadorna in early November and his successor, Armando Diaz, sought to raise army morale by improving soldiers' conditions and providing better weapons. A further result of Caporetto was that the Allies met at Rapallo and set up a War Council to co-ordinate Italian strategy. What this meant in practice was that British and French troops were sent to help on the Italian front – though it is not entirely true that they took over 'the real defence' of the country as Keegan suggests.[33] Even before the reinforcements arrived, the Italian army had rallied. Fighting during November on the slopes of Monte Grappa at the base of the Dolomites, the *Alpini* stubbornly resisted any further incursion on the 'sacred soil' of Italy. Paolo Monelli's battalion, however, was forced to surrender: 'Since we have had nothing to eat or drink for forty hours, and we have no more cartridges, and we are so few, fate closes the act.' He was imprisoned in the Austrian castle of Salzburg, where Christmas brought him 'a host of sad memories'.[34]

Conrad ordered another Austrian attack on 23 December, telling his troops that they would celebrate Christmas in Venice. They took Col de Rosso but an Italian counter-attack recaptured the 4000-foot peak on Christmas Eve. Italians gave thanks for the deliverance of Venice as they took Christmas communion in St Mark's Cathedral; a few feet from its doors a stone marking the spot where an Austrian shell landed in 1917 is a reminder of how close Italy came to defeat in that year.

5 Conclusion

> **KEY ISSUE** How strong was the position of the Central Powers at the end of 1917?

As 1917 came to an end, the Allies had little other than the capture of Jerusalem to celebrate, for the Central Powers seemed to be in the ascendant over most of Europe. German troops still occupied most of Belgium and north-eastern France; much of Russia (including Russian Poland) was in German or Austrian hands; Serbia was held by Austrian and Bulgarian forces; Romania's resources lay at the disposal of Germany; and Austrian soldiers had penetrated far into Italy.

But the outcome of the struggle was not entirely determined by armies fighting for the occupation of territory. Since the beginning of the war the British navy had successfully blockaded the ports of the Central Powers. By this time the inhabitants of Berlin, Vienna, Budapest, Constantinople and Sofia, as well as other towns and cities, were suffering the misery of acute food and fuel shortages; thousands had already died of hunger. Strikes, food riots and Communist unrest were festering. Chapter 5 will examine the role of civilian morale in determining the outcome of this 'total war'.

Military morale could also prove an important factor. Although the Austrian and Turkish armies were still in the field both were riven by nationalist tensions and weakened by inadequate supplies. This chapter has demonstrated their dependence on German help at Gallipoli, in Galicia, on the Isonzo and in Palestine; there was no certainty that Germany could continue to sustain its allies to this extent without risking the exhaustion and demoralisation of its own army.

References

1 Keegan, *First World War*, p. 187.
2 F. Farmborough, *A Nurse at the Russian Front* (Constable, 1974), p. 70.
3 Chickering, *Imperial Germany*, p. 56.
4 Stone, *Eastern Front*, p. 165.
5 O. Figes, *A People's Tragedy* (Jonathan Cape, 1996), pp. 265–6.
6 *Ibid*, p. 281.
7 A. Brusilov, *A Soldier's Notebook* (Macmillan, 1930) p. 282.
8 *Ibid*, p. 290.
9 Farmborough, *Nurse at the Russian Front*, p. 268.
10 A. Knox, *With the Russian Army* (Hutchinson, 1921), Vol. I., pp. 630 & 646.
11 M. Gorky, *Untimely Thoughts* (Garnstone Press, 1970), pp. 76–7.
12 Gilbert, *First World War*, p. 390.
13 I. Hamilton, *Gallipoli Diary* (Edward Arnold, 1920), Vol. I, p. 304.
14 M. Gilbert, *Churchill: A Life* (Heinemann, 1991), pp. 302 & 300.
15 Macdonald, *Voices and Images of the Great War*, pp. 75 & 95.
16 The last three quotations come from N. Steel & P. Hart, *Defeat at Gallipoli* (Macmillan, 1994), pp. 299, 74 & 375.
17 R.J. Crampton, 'The Balkans, 1914–1918' in H. Strachan (ed), *The Oxford Illustrated History of the First World War* (OUP, 1998), p. 69.
18 Lewis, *True Stories*, p. 307.
19 Gilbert, *First World War*, p. 248.
20 M. Harrison, 'The Fight Against Disease in the Mesopotamia Campaign' in Cecil & Liddle, *Armageddon*, p. 479.
21 James, *Imperial Warrior*, p. 176.
22 Lewis, *True Stories*, p. 311.
23 J. Edmunds & H.R. Davies, *Military Operations in Italy* (HMSO, 1949), p. 11.
24 Gilbert, *First World War*, p. 369.
25 Lussu, *Un Anno*, p. 21.
26 *The Great War in Cortina d'Ampezzo* (Cortina d'Ampezzo War Museum, 1997), pp. 9 & 20.
27 Gilbert, *First World War*, p. 166.

28 P. Monelli, *Toes Up*, trans O. Williams (Duckworth, 1930), pp. 87, 59 & 110.
29 Lussu, *Un Anno*, pp. 53 & 113.
30 J. Gooch, 'Morale and Discipline in the Italian Army' in Cecil & Liddle, *Armageddon*, p. 438.
31 Monelli, *Toes Up*, p. 151.
32 R. Absalom, *Italy Since 1800* (Longman, 1995), p. 97.
33 Keegan, *First World War*, p. 445.
34 Monelli, *Toes Up*, pp. 184–7.

Answering essay questions on Chapter 4

Most essay questions on the war can only be answered in the light of its final result and will be discussed at the end of Chapter 6. However, since fighting stopped on the main Eastern Front (Russia) at the end of 1917, some essays involving a comparison between different areas of fighting could be based mainly on the material in Chapters 3 and 4. Two examples will be considered here.

1. What factors enabled most soldiers to carry on fighting in spite of the appalling conditions they faced?

A good way to answer this question is to compare the Western Front, where the mutinies were not persistent, with the Eastern Front, where the Russian army disintegrated in 1917. The challenge is to explain how most soldiers' morale was sustained in spite of the unexpected length of the war, heavy casualties and dreadful conditions. The following factors could be explored and compared:

a) Patriotism could provide clear aims for which to fight: defending the 'sacred soil' of France, avenging the 'atrocities' in Belgium, destroying German 'militarism', 'punishing' England. Such aims were sustained by government propaganda in all the belligerent countries (see pages 88–89). Russian peasant soldiers seem to have felt less bound to the national cause, perhaps because their civilian lives were so hard.

b) Military discipline was clearly important; in all armies there were penalties for desertion and refusal to serve. But too harsh a regime could alienate soldiers, as it did at Etaples in 1917 or in the Italian army before the dismissal of Cadorna. The effects of an absence of military order were apparent in the Russian army after the implementation of Soviet Order Number One.

c) Adequate supplies of food were vital. When the French authorities improved soldiers' diet after the mutinies of 1917 morale improved, as was also the case with Indian troops in Mesopotamia. Lack of food was probably the most important cause of Russian soldiers' disaffection.

d) Drink and tobacco feature strongly in soldiers' letters and memoirs, suggesting that without these drugs they could not have carried on. The vodka ban in Russia had a disastrous effect on soldiers' morale.

e) Sufficient periods of leave and leisure activities for troops were always considered vital by the British and German authorities. The French and Italians found that military spirit improved once they were provided. There is little evidence that the Russian High Command paid attention to such matters.

f) The support of their companions clearly helped French, British and German troops to soldier on. The collapse of the Russian army in 1917 and the Turkish and Austro-Hungarian armies in 1918 could be blamed on nationalist tensions which often ran counter to comradeship.

g) Psychological factors are emphasised in Niall Ferguson's book, *The Pity of War* (1998). He identifies men's pleasure in fighting, the desire to kill their enemies, belief in their own survival and the 'anaesthetic quality of combat'. While such feelings were undoubtedly important it is difficult to understand why they should have kept some armies going and not others.

In conclusion you could question to what extent morale was sustained. In all armies the rate of desertion, self-mutilation, fraternisation with the enemy, grumbling, protest and emotional disorder increased as the war went on. Unless the conditions mentioned above were present to some degree discontent could quickly turn into disintegration – as happened in Russia in 1917. As John Keegan says, 'Every army has a breaking point.'

2. 'One of the major paradoxes of the First World War was that, although the Western Front was the decisive sector, events there were invariably determined by what happened on the Eastern Front.' Discuss this view.

This question invites you engage in the debate over the relative importance of the two fronts, which the combatants themselves found so difficult to resolve. While France and Britain were determined to drive the German invaders out of northern France and Belgium, they sought alternative ways of attacking the enemy. Germany was torn between defending its western conquests and trying to get rid of its eastern enemy. The theory given in the title can be tested with a plan as outlined on p. 70.

You could conclude that events on the Western Front were frequently determined by what was happening in the east.

Nevertheless the judgement given in the title is too simple because it neglects other factors like the naval blockade. It also ignores conscious attempts at a united strategy such as the Chantilly Conference in December 1915.

	Western Front	Eastern Front
1914	German divisions transferred to East – failure of Schlieffen Plan.	← Russian invasion of Germany
1915	Stalemate	→ Gallipoli Campaign Failure of this to break stalemate
1916	Stepping up of offensives, e.g. Somme ← German troops taken from Verdun ←	→ Brusilov offensive
1917		Russian Revolution and collapse of army
1918	← Transfer of most German divisions to the west and decision to launch all-out attack (see page 96).	

Summary Map
The Western, Eastern and Southern Front.

The lines represent the commitment of troops by belligerent countries to the various fronts but not the routes taken.

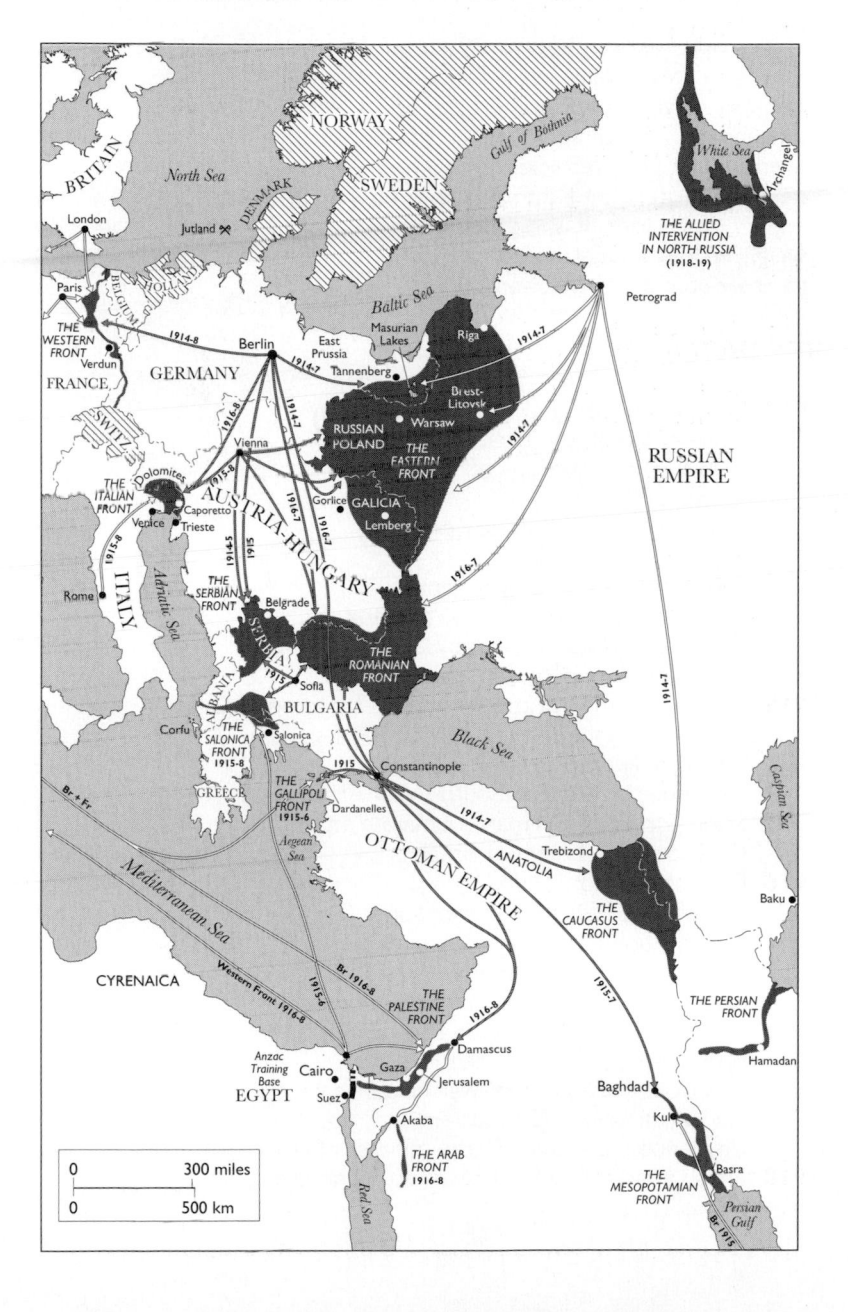

5 Total War

This chapter is an opportunity to explore why some historians use the term 'total war' to describe the First World War.[1] Previous chapters have shown something of its wide geographical scale, its reliance on economic strength, its demand for huge armies – and even its link with genocide. This chapter gives greater dimensions to its global nature and introduces a further aspect of 'total war': its impact on civilians. It should be possible at the end of this chapter to weigh up the importance of the naval conflict and of civilian morale to the outcome of the war.

KEY DATES

1914 Beginning of Allied blockade of Germany
Battle of Heligoland Bight
Two German warships get through Dardanelles
Sinking of *Emden*
German Naval victory at Coronel
Battle of Falkland Islands
Surrender of Kiaochow to Japan
Conquest of Samoa by New Zealand
Conquest of New Guinea by Australia
British attack on German East Africa
1915 German submarine attacks on British and neutral ships
Battle of Dogger Bank
Sinking of *Lusitania*
Surrender of German South-West Africa
Scaling down of German submarine attacks
Coalition government in Britain
1916 Battle of Jutland
Surrender of German Cameroon
Conscription in Britain
'Turnip winter' in Germany
Lloyd George becomes Prime Minister of Britain
1917 Resumption of unrestricted submarine warfare
British use of convoy system
American declaration of war on Germany
Hunger strikes on German ships
Clemenceau becomes Prime Minister of France
1918 British attack on U-boat bases at Zeebrugge

1 Introduction

In November 1914 Britain's First Lord of the Admiralty, Winston Churchill, declared that it was his country's intention to strangle Germany's economy by means of a naval blockade. Two weeks later his German counterpart Admiral Tirpitz announced that Germany would play the same game by sinking British merchant ships. Both the British blockade and German submarine attacks were primarily designed to cause suffering to civilians. They would affect merchant ships as well as warships and neutral countries as well as combatants. Furthermore the campaigns would be waged not only in home waters but on seas far from European shores.

At the same time the war demanded huge effort and sacrifice from civilian workers and families, whose continued support was ensured by means of propaganda. And because the European belligerent countries had overseas empires supplies of men and equipment came also from other continents where, too, blood was shed and livelihoods were affected. So it was that more people than ever before were drawn 'into the cauldron of armed conflict'.[2]

2 Ruling the Waves

KEY ISSUE To what extent did the naval conflict change the course of the war as a whole?

a) The Allied Blockade

Despite the keen naval race between Britain and Germany in the early twentieth century Britannia still ruled the waves (see Table on page 16). Britain's superiority in Dreadnoughts, as well as in the smaller, faster battleships known as cruisers and in submarines, was even more marked when the two alliances were lined up. The addition to British resources of French vessels in the Mediterranean, Russians in the Baltic and Black Sea, Japanese in the Pacific, Italians in the Adriatic and, later, Americans in the Atlantic, created a formidable challenge to the Central Powers. But the alarming toll taken of British and French ships as they entered the Dardanelles in 1915 (see page 58) suggests why the Allies were cautious in the use of their navies. With a large empire as well as vital trade and troop transport routes to protect, the British government dared not risk losing many ships whether to mines and submarines or in a surface battle. As Churchill said, Admiral Jellicoe (who commanded the British Grand Fleet) could lose the war in an afternoon.

Thus, contrary to German expectation, Britain did not adopt a dangerous close blockade of the German coast but rather a distant

blockade from the comparative safety of its naval bases in the Channel
and at Scapa Flow to the north of Scotland. Cruiser patrols, minefields, submarines, nets and searchlights effectively prevented trading
vessels from reaching German ports; it has been estimated that only
642 got through during the whole war.[3] Similar blockades were later
applied to Austria and Turkey with the help of the French, Italian and
Russian navies.

Cut off from imports of food, coal, oil and chemicals, German
people endured cold, hunger and disease. During the winter of
1916–17, the coldest in living memory, the potato crop failed and
turnips became the staple diet; leather was in such short supply that
many resorted to wearing wooden clogs; soap was a rare commodity;
and hot water for bathing was hard to come by. 'The effects of the war
could now be seen, felt, heard, and also smelled.'[4] While most hatred
was reserved for 'one foe alone – England', German anger was
expressed also against fellow countrymen who made a fortune from
the black market and against the government, which made but inept
attempts to manage the shortages. There were frequent food riots
after 1916 and civilian morale was crumbling by 1918. But did
German people actually starve? Historians' answers to this question
range from Peter Loewenberg's claim that 'three quarters of a million
people died of starvation between 1914 and 1918'[5] to Niall Ferguson's
contention that 'the evidence that anyone starved is not to be found'.
The truth must be that the rising civilian death rate (184,896 per
month in 1918 compared to 78,820 in 1913) was due partly to the
'slow starvation' described by contemporaries. While Ferguson is
technically correct in arguing that 'populations have continued to
fight wars despite suffering far greater hunger than that experienced
by Germans in 1918', his description of their plight as one of 'genteel
impoverishment' is a little wide of the mark.[6]

The long blockade also tested the morale of sailors on both sides.
Ship's surgeon, James Shaw, describes efforts to relieve the monotony
of life on board a British patrol cruiser in 1915:

1   15 June: After the novelty of it has worn off one realises how mon-
    strous this patrolling in these vessels is. We see nothing but sea and sky.
    21 June: Ships sports were held today. Tug of war, obstacle race for
    men, officers' obstacle race, potato race, sack race, blindfold boxing,
5   etc.[7]

In the same month German seaman, Richard Stumpf, found
the routine on board his ship even more tedious:

1   On Whitsun Monday we got another uniform inspection. Our
    battle uniforms, in particular, were inspected minutely for dust or spots.
    All those who did not pass had to report for several rounds of punish-
    ment tour. There is now a greater gulf between the officers and the
5   men than at any other period in my naval career. Perhaps once we get
    into action it will all change.[8]

b) Fighting on the High Seas

Stumpf was not alone in longing for the sort of engagements seen in the first few months of the war, when a few fast, well-armed German battlecruisers had kept Allied shipping on the run. Although they were outnumbered by the combined Allied fleets and hampered by the British decoding of their radio messages, these vessels achieved some success in 1914 (see map on page 93).

In August *Goeben* and *Breslau* evaded the French and British to slip through the Dardanelles to Constantinople, where their presence helped to provoke war between Turkey and the Allies. During the autumn *Emden* managed to sink 16 British steamers, a Russian cruiser and a French destroyer in the Indian Ocean before being sunk herself on 9 November. Meanwhile a squadron of five ships commanded by the courageous Admiral Maximilian von Spee had defeated the British at Coronel off the coast of Chile. Outraged at the loss of two heavy cruisers and all their crews (1,600 sailors) in Britain's first naval defeat for a century, the Admiralty sent extra ships to hunt Spee down. They caught him off the Falkland Islands on 8 December, when all but one of the German ships were destroyed. Many lives were lost, and Spee himself was killed.

By 1915 the frustrating stalemate described by Shaw and Stumpf prevailed on the North Sea. After losing four ships at the Battle of Heligoland Bight in August 1914 and another at Dogger Bank in January 1915, the Kaiser was determined not to risk further destruction of his precious navy. Apart from occasional sorties German ships hugged the shore. Later in the year a similar situation developed in the Adriatic, where the Italian navy blockaded Austria while defending its own extensive coastline. It was 'almost as if the Adriatic were a maritime trench across which the two opposing fleets faced each other', writes an Italian historian, pointing to the similarities between the land and sea wars.[9]

The general longing for more 'heroic' naval action was expressed by Vice-Admiral Reinhard Scheer, who assumed command of the German High Seas Fleet in January 1916: 'In this life and death struggle I cannot understand how anyone can think of allowing any weapon which can be used against the enemy to rust in its sheath.'[10] On 31 May 1916 Scheer unsheathed his sword by leading the whole German fleet (including 16 Dreadnoughts and five battlecruisers) out into the North Sea, where he hoped to take the enemy by surprise. With their ability to decode German signals, the British knew these plans were afoot but, because of the Admiralty's faulty transmission of messages, Jellicoe thought that the German battleships were still in harbour. Thus, while sending ahead Admiral Beatty's reconnaissance squadron of cruisers, he advanced more slowly with the Grand Fleet, which included 28 Dreadnoughts. When battle was joined off the Jutland coast of Denmark in mid afternoon, Beatty suffered heavier losses than Scheer. It was only when Jellicoe's battlefleet arrived in the early evening that the balance was reversed. Both sides took heavy punishment but eventually, as a result of overwhelming British fire-power, Scheer had to withdraw. By morning both fleets had returned to their bases. The Kaiser was able to boast that 'the spell of Trafalgar is broken', for the British had lost 14 ships and 6,094 men to the Germans' 11 ships and 2,551 men. On the other hand, the Battle of Jutland had not broken Britain's naval supremacy or control of the North Sea. The British were left in a state of 'bewildered excitement', which is evoked by Vera Brittain, a volunteer army nurse:

1 Were we celebrating a glorious naval victory or lamenting an ignomin-
  ious defeat? We hardly knew. ... The one indisputable fact was that
  hundreds of young men, many of them only just in their teens, had gone
  down without hope of rescue or understanding of the issue to a cold
5 anonymous grave.[11]

c) Submarine Warfare

After the Battle of Jutland the German fleet did not venture out again; now Scheer argued that 'a victorious end to the war can only be achieved ... by using the U-boats [submarines] against British trade'. He knew the risks Germany ran with this method of warfare, for they had been amply demonstrated in the first two years of the war.

The problem did not lie with the weapon itself. Although at the outset Germany had only 24 submarines (to Britain's 78), an intensive construction programme doubled this even by the end of 1914. German submarines were bigger and more powerful than Britain's and could undertake independent offensive operations. They were the ideal vessels from which to launch torpedoes; known to the sailors as 'tin fish', these underwater missiles could sink surface ships in a matter of minutes. At the beginning of 1915, confident in its mastery of this new method of warfare, Germany declared a war zone in which all merchant ships trading with Britain and its allies would be sunk. During that year 396 British and neutral ships were fatally torpedoed.

The risk Germany ran was that this U-boat offensive would so alien-ate neutral countries that they would cut off commercial links or even enter the war on the Allied side. International maritime law required raiders to give merchant ships warning before attacks and to assist in the escape of their crews and passengers. Clearly it was difficult for submarines to abide by these regulations. They were extremely vul-nerable if they spent time on the surface and they did not have the space to take crews aboard. Thus, though U-boat captains were given no specific instructions in 1915, 'naval command proceeded on the assumption that most ships would be torpedoed without warning'.[12] In practice, historians find, 'the record of German submariners was overwhelmingly honourable given the limitations of their operational

circumstances'.[13] There is evidence of their towing lifeboats, adminis-
tering first aid and offering food and wine to survivors. Such measures
were not sufficient, however, to deflect the rage of neutral countries
when their ships were sunk or their subjects drowned. On 7 May 1915
America was outraged when a Cunard liner, *Lusitania,* on its journey
from New York to Liverpool, was torpedoed without warning off the
Irish coast. Sinking all the more rapidly because of the contraband
ammunition in its hold, it took down 1,201 passengers, of whom 128
were American. This led to a crisis in Germany's relations with the
USA; after receiving a series of strongly-worded notes from President
Wilson, Berlin ordered that submarine action should in future abide
by maritime law.

In the ensuing months furious arguments raged between German
political leaders, anxious to avoid conflict with America, and naval
commanders, desperate to challenge Britain's control of the sea.
After the frustrations of Jutland and Verdun, Hindenburg and
Ludendorff added to the pressure on the German government which,
on 1 February 1917, announced the resumption of 'unrestricted submarine warfare'. During the first half of 1917 the campaign came
close to success with an average of 242.8 Allied and neutral ships
being sunk each month. Among them was the transport ship *Arcadian*
carrying 18-year-old Trooper Reginald Huggins and 'a full comple-
ment of cannon fodder' to the eastern fronts. Unlike most of his companions, he was able to don a life-belt and to escape by means of a
rope, thus surviving to recall his terrifying experience:

1   Being a non-swimmer at that time, I was unable to get clear of the ship,
    and her enormous bulk seemed likely to topple over upon me at any
    moment, supposing I was not sucked down one of the huge funnels by
    the inrush of water. ... The suspense, fortunately, was brief. For a
5   moment or two the *Arcadian* partly righted on her keel and then with
    much hissing from the boiler rooms, she slid for ever out of sight of
    human eyes, carrying with her hundreds of troops and her own crew
    caught like rats on the lower decks. Within three minutes from the
    time that she was struck all that remained of the ship was bits of float-
10 ing wreckage.

Huggins spent the night on a raft 'in the excellent company of five
officers' and was picked up by a rescue ship the next day.[14]

The British Admiralty devised some moderately successful strat-
egies to avoid such disasters: disguising armed ships as merchant
vessels (Q-ships), painting ships with 'dazzle' camouflage, mining the
exits from U-boat bases and diverting shipping away from danger
zones. But until late April 1917 the system of sending merchant ships
in convoys escorted by destroyers was rejected as too hazardous. On
28 April the first convoy sailed and reached Britain safely; from then
on the system was gradually introduced, with the result that losses of
merchant ships declined to 147.8 a month in the second part of the

year. At the same time Germany was losing more submarines than it could replace (66 in 1917). By the end of 1917 the U-boat campaign was affecting British civilians, who had now to accept rationing, but it was not starving the country into submission. Germany had been defeated in the economic war.

Disastrously, it had also lost the diplomatic war. The combination of further attacks on American shipping and a clumsy attempt to persuade Mexico to declare war on the USA brought even the peace-loving President Wilson to a declaration of war in April 1917. Seaman Stumpf was convinced that 'we need not trouble ourselves too much' about 'Yankee' battleships. He was misinformed. The first and the most important effect of American intervention was to strengthen Allied efforts at sea. Modern American warships helped to escort convoys and to enforce the blockade of the Central Powers. Germany stood no chance now of turning the tide in the sea war.

During 1918 U-boats did progressively less damage to Allied trade and troop movements. However, sailing remained perilous; even hospital ships were liable to attack. In June 1918, for instance, 283 patients and 91 medical staff died when *Llandovery Castle* was blown up. The main naval action of the year was a futile British attack on U-boat bases at Zeebrugge and Ostend. This achieved little apart from providing participants like Seaman W. Wainwright with a release for 'all the pent-up feeling of the years of war and hatred'.[15]

For German sailors still marooned in North Sea bases there was no such escape from monotony. Tension between officers and men mounted, erupting during the summer of 1917 in the form of hunger strikes and insubordination. Two ringleaders were shot and others were given harsh prison sentences, while on the other hand seamen now got 'plenty of food'. Neither the stick nor the carrot seems to have worked; bitterness continued to simmer and Seaman Stumpf was convinced that 'an actual revolutionary situation exists in the fleet'.[16] Events in October–November 1918 were to prove him right (see page 109).

d) The Importance of the Naval War

Battles on land could often be heard and even smelt three miles out at sea. Conversely the naval conflict affected most spheres of land warfare. The Allies could transport their troops to most fronts and could bring colonial recruits to fight in Europe, albeit at some risk. On the other hand, the blocking of one narrow sea passage, the Dardanelles, made it impossible for Britain and France to support the Russian army. The Italian navy played a useful role in rescuing the Serbian army in 1915 and in firing on Austrian troops when they threatened Venice in 1917. On the Western Front the early battles of Ypres were fought largely to prevent Germany from gaining more Channel ports and the third battle there in 1917 had German U-boat bases as its abortive goal. Most crucially, Germany's desperate submarine offensive drew the United States into the war, thus revitalising Allied efforts on the Western Front in 1918. (See pages 96–99.)

Civilians as well as soldiers were affected by maritime events. Hundreds of residents in coastal towns, like Scarborough and Whitby on the North Sea or Ancona on the Adriatic, were killed or injured by naval bombardment. Ships' crews and passengers were always in peril. 14,287 seafarers on British ships alone lost their lives – though such was the cosmopolitan nature of the crews that 40 per cent of those killed were not natively British. Most civilians suffered the effects of naval blockade; in Central Power countries deprivation was serious enough to help cause their collapse in October–November 1918.

Finally the sailors themselves should not be forgotten. Their overall casualty rate was much lower than that of soldiers but seamen were in constant danger; when a ship went down it was often 'with all hands'. The battleship *Vanguard* blew up at Scapa Flow in July 1918 killing 804, exceeding the number of Britons who died in gas attacks during the whole war.[17] But who now remembers *Vanguard* as the victims of gas are remembered? The dullness and tensions of life at sea could lead to low morale. Sailors' testimony suggests that this could be averted where officers took care to run a 'happy ship' but that these human factors were largely neglected in the German navy. The unrest which erupted on ships and in ports in 1918 had no small effect on the war's outcome.

3 Competing for 'Places in the Sun'

> **KEY ISSUE** How important was the contribution of their colonies to the Allies' war against Germany?

In spite of entering late into the European competition for colonies, Germany had gained a sizeable overseas empire by 1914: extensive, though not very productive, lands in Africa, strategically placed islands in the Pacific and the commercial area of Kiaochow on the Chinese coast. Lack of naval power meant that Germany could not easily defend its colonial garrisons. Britain and France, on the other hand, could depend on Asian and African recruits and resources throughout the war. Other participants such as Japan, Australia and New Zealand, hoped to gain territory as a reward for helping the Allies, and Germany's colonies proved to be useful bargaining counters (see map on page 93).

a) Asia

Soon after entering the war in August 1914 Japan attacked Germany's

Asiatic possessions. By October it had occupied most of German's islands in the central Pacific and was besieging the heavily fortified garrison at Kiaochow. 3,000 German marines fought desperately against 50,000 Japanese troops before surrendering on 7 November. Meanwhile Germany had not been able to prevent a New Zealand force from taking Samoa or an Australian battalion from overcoming New Guinea. By the end of the year Germany had lost its Asiatic colonies, which Britain now pledged to their various conquerors (see page 20).

These campaigns had not greatly affected the colonies' inhabitants. Britain's Indian subjects, however, were heavily involved in the war even though there was no fighting there. Of nearly one and a half million volunteer troops 113,743 fell as casualties and 12 won the Victoria Cross, the highest award for bravery. In addition India produced vital military supplies (such as jute for sandbags) and contributed to war loans. Abnormal price rises affected most Indian people. At first there was genuine loyal support coupled with an expectation that India's help would bring its reward in the form of dominion status (full self-government such as was enjoyed by Canada, Australia and New Zealand). But after two years many Indians became weary of participating in a distant war whose conduct they could not influence. Recruitment drives and demands for loans met with some resistance and the nationalist movement (Indian National Congress) gained support. Dependent as it was on Indian help, the British government promised in 1917 that the war would be followed by:

> not only the increasing association of Indians in every branch of the administration but also the granting of self-governing institutions with the view to a progressive realisation of responsible government in India as an integral part of the British Empire.

Such cautious pledges were not well-received in India, particularly as they were accompanied by repressive security regulations. It is no accident that an independence campaign followed the war; its leader, Mohandas Gandhi, had earlier helped with recruiting campaigns but was now convinced that 'India had been tricked into giving her support to Britain's war'.[18]

b) Africa

The Allies decided early in the war to attack Germany's African colonies, which contained important radio stations and military bases. In August 1914 Togoland was forced to surrender to troops of the West African Frontier Force commanded by British and French officers. In Cameroon 1,000 German and 3,000 African soldiers put up more determined resistance, retreating inland after the British captured the ports, capital and radio station. A difficult campaign resulted in the surrender of the last German garrison in March 1916 (see picture on page 83). For the conquest of German South-West Africa Britain relied on the South African army composed largely of Boers (Dutch-speaking white South Africans) against whom they had only recently fought. A Boer rebellion had to be crushed before the campaign could get under way in January 1915. German resistance was overcome by July of the same year.

In German East Africa, however, conflict lasted from when the British first attacked, on 8 August 1914, until 23 November 1918 – after the armistice in Europe. This was partly because it was the most valuable of Germany's colonies and partly because the leader of its forces here, Colonel Lettow-Vorbeck, was a particularly determined and skilful soldier. With about 2,500 local troops (known as *askaris*) and 200 white officers he defeated several British and Indian expeditionary forces, capturing vast supplies of their weapons and ammunition in the process, and then conducted fierce guerrilla warfare. By the end the British had recruited over 30,000 African troops for this arduous campaign in the bush, which exerted a high toll of death through disease. Because this part of Africa was infested with a type of tsetse fly deadly to pack-animals and had no roads suitable for vehicles, a million or so human porters were used for the transport of weapons, ammunition, food and water.

Such evidence as exists suggests that it was not difficult for either side to recruit African troops, who were paid at least three times more than local wage rates. They seem, too, to have felt loyalty to the cause of their European rulers. A Senegalese veteran told a French historian in 1972 that to West Africans 'France's victory meant our victory'.[19] In supporting the European war and encouraging recruitment, educated Africans, like Blaise Diagne, the first black deputy to the French National Assembly, hoped to gain more rights and recognition. Some warrior tribes welcomed the opportunity to practise their skills – though this enthusiasm was not always acceptable to their white rulers, as is shown by Karen Blixen, a Danish woman living in British East Africa:

1 When the Great War first broke out, and the Masai had news of it, the
   blood of the old fighting tribe was all up. They had visions of splendid
   battles and massacres and they saw the glory of their past returning
   once more. ... But the English government did not think it wise to
5 organize the Masai to make war on white men, be they even Germans,
   and it forbade the Masai to fight, and put an end to all their hopes.

When, however, the colonial powers introduced conscription, calling up Africans to serve either as combatant troops in Europe (as the French did) or as porters (as all the Europeans did) there was widespread resistance and resentment. After all, the slave trade was not very far in the past.

Despite raising their hopes the war did not bring black African people political rights, even in West Africa where a few African nominees were admitted to legislative councils. In the European settler colonies and in South Africa whites actually strengthened their position. After the war Germany's former colonies were allocated to Britain, France and South Africa, though it is true that they were to be called mandates, with the idea that the rulers were trustees responsible for the interests of native inhabitants (see page 122). More immediate recognition for African participation in the war came in the form of medals. A ceremony awarding them to Masai chiefs, who had eventually been allowed to scout for the British, is described by Karen Blixen without any ironic intention:

1 Berkeley [the British representative] took out the medals, solemnly reading out, one after another, the names of the Masai chiefs, and handing them their medals with a generously outstretched arm. The Masai took them from him very silently, in an outstretched hand. ... A medal
5 is an inconvenient thing to give to naked man, because he has got no place to fix it on to, and the old Masai chiefs kept standing with theirs in their hand. After a time a very old man came up to me, held out his hand with the medal in it, and asked me to tell him what it had got on it. I explained it to him as well as I could. The silver coin had on the one
10 side a head of Britannia, and upon the other side the words: 'The Great War for Civilization.'[20]

4 Keeping the Home Fires Burning

KEY ISSUE How important was the support and participation of civilians to the war as a whole?

Keep the home fires burning
While your hearts are yearning
Though the lads are far away,
They dream of home. ...

... sang homesick British soldiers in the trenches. And servicemen of other nationalities had similarly sentimental songs to remind them of home. The millions of letters exchanged between civilians and servicemen linked the home and the fighting fronts still more closely – as all military censors were aware. In the case of Russia, overworked government censors worried (with good reason) that information received in letters from home in 1916–17 was helping to demoralise soldiers:

1 One cannot help but notice that in letters from the army as well as, mainly, in letters to the army, discontent arising from the internal political situation of the country is beginning to grow. ... Rumours about disorders and strikes at factories are reaching the army and these
5 rumours, often exaggerated and embroidered, cause depression in the soldiers' morale and much worry about the fate of relatives at home.[21]

Burning a native village in German Cameroon.

This section examines the part played in the war by families, civilian workers (including women) and politicians in the other Entente countries and in the Central Powers.

a) Physical Factors: Death and Devastation

To modern readers this aspect of war is all too obvious as nations still send armies to invade neighbouring territories and television reveals the havoc and destruction they cause to both land and inhabitants. Britons in 1914 were as shocked by Germany's treatment of the Belgian population and the ravaging of places like the historic university town of Louvain as they have been in recent years by the fate of Bosnians and the city of Sarajevo at the hands of the Serbs. In Allied propaganda Belgian 'atrocities' tended to be exaggerated; lurid stories were told, for instance, of nuns being hanged from bell towers. Recent research confirms that this was indeed a harsh period in the life of Belgium, and some historians claim that it was 'even harsher than that of the Nazi occupation 30 years later'.[22] Male and female mortality rates rose by 160 and 127 per cent respectively during the war as a result of malnutrition and disease as well as the fighting. To avoid such calamities many Belgians fled; a quarter of a million came to England, for instance, where they were initially greeted with enthusiasm – they even helped to inspire the creation of Agatha Christie's detective-hero, Hercule Poirot. As so often happens, sympathy with the refugees soon began to wane: trade unions worried that these industrious foreigners might compete for jobs; landlords suspected that they would be noisy and excitable lodgers; and Welsh Nonconformists were shocked when Roman Catholics attended their local chapels.[23]

In other war zones, too, civilians were forced from their homes by advancing troops: Russians fled from Germans, Austrians from Russians, Italians from Austrians, Serbs from Bulgarians, Caucasian Russians from Turks ... the list grew as the war went on. The English nurse, Florence Farmborough, epitomised the plight of all such displaced people when she described:

> a sad procession [of Austrian refugees] ... helpless multitudes, driven from their native villages and forced willy-nilly into strange surroundings under a strange, hostile government.[24]

As the French historian Annette Becker writes of German-occupied northern France: 'in occupied territory war is total war'. She uses the diary kept by David Hirsch, a shopkeeper in Roubaix, to illustrate the miseries of the subject population: a complete absence of news from the front or communication with the rest of France (even by carrier pigeon); chronic food shortages; the billeting of German soldiers in their homes; the requisitioning of domestic articles and industrial products; compulsory payments and forced labour. From areas which did not co-operate hostages were taken and sent to 'concentration camps' and anyone (like the English nurse Edith Cavell) found to be helping Allied soldiers to escape from the occupied zone was charged with espionage and executed. It was small consolation that such 'excessive' demands were 'proof of the shortages which must exist in Germany itself'. Unknown to Hirsch, the occupation of these ten valuable départements did much to stiffen French determination to defeat the hated enemy. To this day French writing on this subject is far from dispassionate; Becker herself suggests that French suffering in this area was akin to that of the Armenians massacred by the Turks (see page 58).[25]

For civilian populations further away from the fighting destruction might come from bombs dropped by Zeppelins or, later in the war, by newly-developed bomber planes. Both the sight of the giant airships and the noise of the aeroplanes (which sounded like tractors in the sky) aroused terror among the inhabitants of French, German and British cities. Several thousands were killed or injured by bombs. Nevertheless, these aerial attacks on civilians were not a crucial factor in this war as they were to be in later conflicts. Towns and buildings were more likely to be flattened by land bombardment than by air raids – as is typified by the fate of the fine Flemish wool town of Ypres, the scene of three Western Front battles.

b) Political Factors: Personalities and Policies

The ability of civilian populations to withstand the strains of war depended largely on the lead and support given by governments. A comparison of British, French and German politics will suggest the difference which such factors could make.

In each of these countries most politicians of all parties put aside their differences at the beginning of the war. The French Prime Minister, Viviani, created the *Union Sacrée*, a 'coalition of national defence'. The leaders of the Conservative, Irish and Labour parties made a truce to support the British Liberal Prime Minister, Asquith. In the German Reichstag even deputies of the revolutionary Social Democratic Party responded to the Kaiser's claim that the war 'recognised no parties, only Germans' by giving their unanimous backing to Chancellor Bethmann Hollweg. When the war carried on beyond the expected few months' duration, however, cracks began to appear in these fragile political structures.

The indecisive Viviani resigned in October 1914. His successor, Aristide Briand, managed better than he had to exercise some control over French military commanders but was forced to leave office after the disasters of 1917 (see page 45). Two further prime ministers followed in quick succession amid scandals involving the sale of Allied secrets to Germany. Meanwhile the Socialists demanded a negotiated peace and abandoned the *Union Sacrée*. It was only when President Poincaré reluctantly promoted his erstwhile political enemy, the 76-year-old 'Tiger' Clemenceau, in November 1917 that France found the prime minister it needed at an exceptionally difficult time. A brilliant journalist as well as a Radical politician, Clemenceau had fiercely criticised previous governments for their conduct of the war. Now he voiced his dedication to a victory to avenge the defeat of 1871, which he well remembered. With his frequent visits to the front line (where a soldier gave him a bunch of chalk-dusted flowers which stand on the desk in his Paris apartment to this day), his rousing speeches which were pinned up in village halls and his taming of the High Command, Clemenceau carried the nation behind him – though he was never without opposition in the Assembly. It is tempting to suggest that Winston Churchill learned something from his robust leadership; for Churchill was present in April 1918 when Clemenceau expressed French determination to resist the Germans' spring offensive which threatened the capital: 'I will fight in front of Paris, I will fight in Paris, I will fight behind Paris.' 'Everyone knew', commented Churchill, 'that this was no idle boast.'[26]

Churchill's own war career reflected the political turmoil of the time. A member of Asquith's War Council in 1914, he resigned in 1915 during the unsuccessful Gallipoli campaign (see pages 57–60), which also forced Asquith to form a Coalition government consisting of Liberal, Conservative and Labour ministers. The frustrated

Churchill soon went off to fight on the Western Front. During 1916 the Prime Minister was demoralised by further difficulties: the political struggles over conscription, the republican Easter Rising in Dublin, the drowning at sea of Lord Kitchener and the death of his son Raymond in the Battle of the Somme. Criticism of his lackadaisical leadership culminated in an ultimatum from his Minister of Munitions, Lloyd George, in which he threatened to 'leave the Government in order to inform the people of the real condition of affairs, and to give them an opportunity, before it is too late, to save their native land from a disaster'.[27] The result was Asquith's resignation and Lloyd George's appointment as head of a new Coalition government, which soon included Churchill as Minister of Munitions. Lloyd George was to bring new vigour to the conduct of the war and, like Clemenceau, he won the confidence of the people, though never that of Haig, with whom he sparred continuously over strategy.

There were no such struggles in Germany, where Bethmann Hollweg tended to give way to all military demands and the Reichstag delegated its legislative powers to the non-elected Bundesrat. By 1916 the Chancellor was beginning to favour a negotiated peace but, under the increasingly dominant leadership of Paul von Hindenburg (Head of Supreme Command) and Erich Ludendorff (Commander-in-Chief), this was never a possibility. These two men formed a virtual military dictatorship, Hindenburg providing the 'charismatic authority' and Ludendorff the 'ferocious energy and willpower'.[28] In the Reichstag, however, opposition grew and it actually dared to pass a Peace Resolution in July 1917. A trial of strength ensued, which resulted in the dismissal of Bethmann Hollweg. His successor, the High Command's nominee Georg Michaelis, was sacked four months later when the Reichstag defied the government again with a resolution calling for suffrage reform. Bitter debate continued to rage in the Reichstag under the new Chancellor, Count von Hertling, but it was snuffed out by Germany's victory in the east and Ludendorff's expansionist Treaty of Brest-Litovsk, both of which were widely celebrated. Until the failure of Germany's offensive in the summer of 1918 (see pages 99–103) Hindenburg and Ludendorff ruled Germany, often without reference to the Kaiser himself.

Through all these changes governments took on increasing powers to meet the unanticipated demands of the long war. Britain would not have been able to engage so actively on the Western and Eastern Fronts had it not introduced conscription in 1916. Nor would Lloyd George have met the pressing demand for munitions without an unprecedented direction of labour. Coming to the conclusion that 'the greatest of [Britain's] deadly foes is Drink', he also brought in greater controls over the sale of alcohol; no one, for instance was allowed to treat anyone else to a drink. Successive governments were reluctant to regulate Britain's food supply, but eventually rationing was enforced in 1918 in the face of Germany's attacks on merchant shipping. To help make these sacrifices (as well as soaring casualty rates) acceptable there were also such palliative measures as separation allowances, rent control and housing subsidies.

France, possessing a smaller population and having lost a high proportion of its industrial resources, faced even greater strains and increasingly depended on its ally across the Channel. To produce sufficient armed forces to fight Germany it recruited 67 per cent of adult males – and then recalled half a million of them to man essential factories. Unlike Britain, which already had relatively high levels of income tax, France introduced direct taxation as a war measure and still had to meet four-fifths of its costs by borrowing and printing money, which caused dangerously high levels of inflation. The early provision of generous separation allowances, a moratorium on rents and the curtailment of employers' war profits eased the strain to some extent; and there seems to have been no attempt to curb French consumption of wine.

Germany's response to the emergency created by prolonged land fighting and the British blockade was the Hindenburg Programme for the total concentration of resources on arms production. Non-essential industries were closed down, employers were paid high prices for war products and all male Germans between 17 and 60 were conscripted into war service. By means of this massive bureaucratic intervention (as well as ruthless exploitation of the occupied territories), the army was well supplied with weapons and munitions. The government understood civilian needs less well. For example, in an attempt to relieve the grain shortage it ordered the slaughter of nine million pigs, thus depriving people of an essential source of food and manure. Profiteering, the black market and prices went uncontrolled while there were few policies to alleviate hardship. The German government's priorities are illustrated by the fact that it spent 83 per cent of its budget on military needs and only two per cent on civilians; corresponding percentages for Britain were 62 and 16.[29]

c) Social Factors: Mass Mobilisation and Morale

The war demanded a great deal from families. Nine million men – fathers, husbands, sons, brothers, cousins and friends – never returned and a further 18 million came back maimed. In addition those left behind had to pay for and make the weapons used at the front and to put up with the shortages and high prices caused by economic warfare. 'War seeped into every corner of society: no one was free of it; no one was safe.'[30]

As the previous section suggested, many civilians were required for the urgent production of raw materials, machines and food. In fact, for many families these added employment opportunities and increased wages brought greater prosperity. The war did not bring only loss. All the participant countries had to depend on women to substitute for workers who had been called up, to produce munitions and other war requirements and to support the armed services by nursing, clerical work, catering and driving – only in Russia did some women actually fight. The women who took up these roles often moved from low-paid 'women's work' such as dressmaking or domestic service or returned to work similar to that which they had done before they were married. There is much oral evidence to suggest that they welcomed the chance to do their bit in the war. But in all countries these vital women workers were paid less than their male counterparts and were made to understand that their jobs would only last as long as the war (see also pages 135–137).

The temporary 'dilution' of labour (in which jobs were broken down into tasks requiring less skill) had the agreement of the trade unions, which acceded to a general industrial truce in 1914. The truce did not last out the war, however. The last two years saw strikes by British miners, shipworkers and munitions workers, by French clothing workers, masons, railwaymen, miners and munitions workers and by German industrial workers of all kinds. The strikers usually complained about the high cost of living and profiteering. In France and Britain conciliation and concessions brought an end to most stoppages while in Germany, where the situation was more threatening, the leaders were imprisoned and the strikers were sent to the front.

The most serious unrest (apart from that in Russia) occurred in Austrian cities where the government's reduction of the flour ration in January 1918 caused a wave of strikes and riots. This is a clue to the greatest advantage enjoyed by French and British civilians – that their governments were able to guarantee food supplies. Population statistics, while revealing a catastrophic rise in mortality rates for young men in all combatant countries, show improved survival rates for women and older men in France and Britain – until the flu epidemic of 1918. Nutrition standards actually improved in both countries. In Germany and Austria, on the other hand, blockade and mismanagement led to higher mortality for all age groups throughout the war. There is also oral evidence of distress: Viennese residents recall queuing for hours, scavenging for food and fuel, relying on turnips as a staple diet, constant hunger and freezing cold. These contrasting material conditions help to explain the maintenance of Allied civilian morale and the exhaustion which was sapping German and Austrian stamina by 1918.

d) Psychological Factors: Propaganda and Pacifism

Another important factor in keeping up morale was the propaganda issued by governments and independent agencies. This took the form of suppressing undesirable information and of creating positive messages to justify the nation's cause. Propaganda entered every home in the form of newspapers, leaflets, picture postcards and objects rang-ing from Kitchener or Hindenburg beer mugs to French children's board games. At the cinema and music hall performers like Charlie Chaplin and Harry Lauder urged audiences to love their country and hate the enemy, as did leaders of the community such as teachers and clergymen. Posters adorned the walls of every combatant nation. It is, of course, very difficult to know how much psychological effect all this had. Common sense – and academic historians – would suggest that propaganda only stuck when it confirmed what people already felt and that we patronise our forbears if we see them as easy dupes of the media. Peter Liddle's research, for instance, shows that there was much spontaneous loyalty among soldiers and civilians.[31] J.-J. Becker finds that French people broadly accepted the war 'because they were part of one nation'.[32] Most Germans undoubtedly felt genuine pride in their noble *Kultur*. Ordinary citizens everywhere felt that they must stick by the war (as the song promised) 'till the boys come home'.

A few, on the other hand, campaigned for peace. In Britain some Socialists and Nonconformists opposed the war from the start. They often went on to support the Non-Conscription Fellowship (N.C.F.) formed at the end of 1914, arguing that human life was sacred and that governments had no right to compel anyone to bear arms. In spite of having 200 branches by the end of 1915, the N.C.F. was unable to prevent the enforcement of conscription or to stop the war. However, Britain was the only country (apart from the USA after 1917) to recognise the right to object to military service on conscientious grounds. Of the 16,000 who claimed exemption from fighting only 1,500 were 'absolute' objectors who refused to do any kind of war service and received prison sentences. Thus those described by the *Evening Standard*, after an N.C.F. meeting addressed by Bertrand Russell in 1916, as 'hordes of cowards', presented no challenge to Britain's prosecution of the war and there was no real need to treat them so harshly.[33]

Similarly few French men or women questioned the need for the country to defend itself. There was little support for the anti-war sentiments expressed by writers like Romain Rolland, who had to work in Switzerland. The revolutionary trade union leader Clovis Andrieu organised several short-lived anti-war strikes of Loire metal workers early in 1918 but after his imprisonment the movement died down. If pacifism carried risks in Britain and France it was almost impossible in Germany, where the censors were even more vigilant. In private homes and clubs, however, 'nihilist' readings, poetry and cabaret songs expressed the idea of war as an utter absurdity. This *avant-garde* circle consisted of no more than a few hundred people. But with the deterioration in material conditions more open disaffection developed. Thousands gathered on May Day 1916 to hear the Socialist leader Karl Liebknecht shout 'Down with the War! Down with the Government!' before he was arrested and sentenced to four years' imprisonment. The German strikes of 1917–18 were more pacifist than those in France and had more support. Nevertheless Ludendorff had no more difficulty in dealing with the strikes and with the Reichstag Peace Resolution than the naval authorities had in crushing sailors' mutinies in 1917. Most German people now struggled on.

5 Conclusion

Austrian soldiers serving on the Italian front in January 1918 were so ravenous that they regularly dug up maggot-ridden meat which had been declared inedible and buried. Longing to get their hands on Allied supplies of food, wine and tobacco, they pleaded 'for an immediate offensive so that they would not die of hunger'.[34] Such stories illustrate how the various aspects of 'total war' interacted with each other.

For it was the naval blockade which was most responsible for sapping the strength of both troops and civilians in all the Central Powers – although the troops quoted above do not seem to have lacked fighting spirit. Failure in the sea war had also deprived them of any support they might have gained from Germany's overseas possessions. Above all it had brought them a new enemy, the United States, which dramatically tipped the balance of economic strength in the Allies' favour (see table on page 110).

But this economic inferiority should not blind us to the possibility of a German victory. Its strong hold over Belgium and northern France, its victory over Russia and the prospect of rich gains in Eastern Europe, its firm military leadership and the enduring patriotism of its people were all factors which could have proved decisive in 1918.

References

1   E.g. S. Tucker, *The Great War* (UCL Press, 1998), p. 205. Tucker applies the term also to the American Civil War. Other historians claim that the First World War was 'the first of its kind': Winter & Baggett, *Great War*, p. 107.
2   Winter & Baggett, *Great War*, p. 107.
3   C. Page, 'The British Experience of Enforcing Blockade' in Cecil & Liddle, *Armageddon*, p. 137.
4   Chickering, *Imperial Germany*, p. 141.
5   P. Loewenberg, 'Germany, the Home Front' in Cecil & Liddle, *Armageddon*, p. 556.
6   Ferguson, *Pity of War*, pp. 277–80.
7   P. Liddle, *The Sailor's War* (Blandford Press, 1985), p. 92.
8   D. Horn (ed), *The Private World of Seaman Stumpf* (Leslie Frewin, 1969), pp. 97–8.
9   R. Sicurezza, 'Italy and the War in the Adriatic' in Cecil & Liddle, *Armageddon*, p. 182.
10   Keegan, *First World War*, p. 290.
11   V. Brittain, *Testament of Youth* (Victor Gollancz, 1933) p. 192.
12   W. Rahn, 'The German Naval War: Strategy and Experience' in Cecil & Liddle, *Armageddon*, pp. 124 & 126.

13 T. Lane, 'The British Merchant Seaman at War' in *Ibid.* p. 148.
14 Lewis, *True Stories*, pp. 407–9.
15 *Ibid*, p. 404.
16 Horn, *Private World*, pp. 348–56.
17 Gilbert, *First World War*, p. 347.
18 M. Edwardes, *Asia in the European Age* (Thames & Hudson, 1961), pp. 212 & 214.
19 B. Waites, 'Peoples of the Underdeveloped World' in Cecil & Liddle, *Armageddon*, p. 605.
20 Both quotations from K. Blixen, *Out of Africa* (Penguin, 1954), pp. 198 & 201.
21 I. Davidian, 'The Russian Soldier's Morale from the Evidence of Tsarist Military Censorship' in Cecil & Liddle, *Armageddon*, p. 432.
22 R. Wall & J. Winter, *The Upheaval of War* (CUP, 1988), p. 26.
23 B. Turner, *Dear Old Blighty* (Michael Joseph, 1980), pp. 81–4.
24 Farmborough, *Nurse at the Russian Front*, pp. 201–2.
25 A. Becker, 'Life in an Occupied Zone: Lille, Roubaix, Tourcoing' in Cecil & Liddle, *Armageddon*, pp. 630–42.
26 G. Dallas, *At the Heart of a Tiger* (Macmillan, 1993), p. 532.
27 P. Adelman, *The Decline of the Liberal Party* (Longman, 1995), p. 81.
28 Chickering, *Imperial Germany*, pp. 73–5.
29 Tucker, *Great War*, p. 206.
30 Winter & Baggett, *Great War*, p. 107.
31 P. Liddle, 'British Loyalties: The Evidence of an Archive' in Cecil & Liddle, *Armageddon*, pp. 529–536.
32 J.-J. Becker, *The Great War and the French People*, trans. A. Pomerans (Berg, 1985), p. 327.
33 K. Robbins, 'The British Experience of Conscientious Objection' in Cecil & Liddle, *Armageddon*, p. 698.
34 Herwig, *The First World War*, p. 365.

Structured questions on Chapter 5

a) In what ways did the naval war affect civilians? (*10 marks*)
b) For what other reasons did the First World War have a significant impact on civilians? (*10 marks*)
c) To what extent does civilian involvement in the First World War justify the description 'Total War'? (*20 marks*)

Source-based questions on Chapter 5

Read the extracts about colonial warfare by the British government (page 80) and Karen Blixen (pages 81 & 82) and look at the picture on page 83.

a) What is meant by the following terms:
 i) 'self-governing institutions' (line 2 on page 80 in extract). (*2 marks*)
 ii) 'Great War for Civilisation' (line 11 on page 82 in extract). (*2 marks*)

b) What aspects of the British government's promise of 1917 would have disappointed Indian leaders? (*4 marks*)
c) How useful are the two stories told by Karen Blixen for revealing British attitudes towards their African subjects? (*6 marks*)
d) A.J.P. Taylor used the caption 'Civilisation comes to Africa' for the picture of an African village. How justified was his irony in the light of these sources and your knowledge of the colonial war? (*10 marks*)

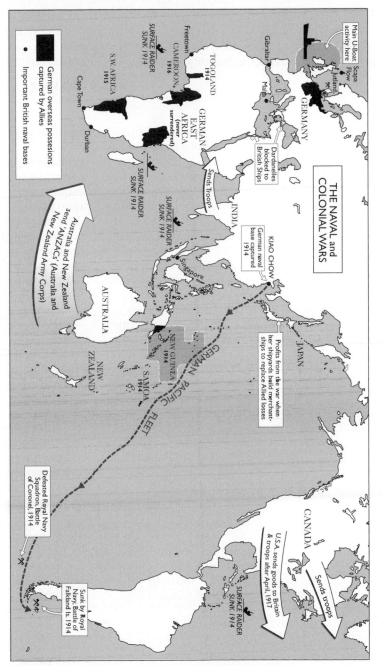

Summary Map
The War at Sea.

THE NAVAL and
COLONIAL WARS

Main U-Boat
activity here

Scapa
Flow

Jutland

GERMANY

Gibraltar

Malta

Dardanelles
blocked to
British Ships

Freetown

CAMEROON
1916

SURFACE RAIDER
SUNK 1914

TOGOLAND
1914

S.W. AFRICA
1915

GERMAN
EAST
AFRICA
(never
surrendered)

Cape Town

Durban

Sends Troops

INDIA

Singapore

KIAO CHOW

German naval
base captured
1914

Profits from the war when
her shipyards build merchant-
ships to replace Allied losses

SURFACE RAIDER
SUNK 1914

SURFACE RAIDER
SUNK 1914

Australia and New Zealand
send 'ANZACs' (Australia and
New Zealand Army Corps)

AUSTRALIA

JAPAN

GERMAN
NEW GUINEA
1914

NEW
ZEALAND

SAMOA
1914

GERMAN PACIFIC FLEET

CANADA

U.S.A. sends goods to Britain
& troops after April, 1917

Sends troops

SURFACE RAIDER
SUNK 1914

Defeated Royal Navy
Squadron, Battle
of Coronel, 1914

Sunk by Royal
Navy, Battle of
Falkland Is. 1914

German overseas possesions
captured by Allies

Important British naval bases

6 The Final Stages of the War: 1918

This chapter describes the changing fortunes of participant countries during the last year of the war. As you read it try to place yourself in that year and to understand that the defeat of Germany was anything but certain. Look out for the factors which explain the Allied victory.

KEY DATES: 1918

3 March	Treaty of Brest-Litovsk
21 March	Operation 'Michael'
9 April	Operation 'Georgette'
7 May	Treaty of Bucharest
26 May	Third German Offensive (The Aisne)
15 July	Last German Offensive (The Marne)
8 August	Beginning of Allied Counter-Offensive (Amiens)
29 September	Ludendorff's decision to seek armistice
30 September	Bulgarian armistice
1 October	Allied conquest of Damascus
3 October	Ludendorff's letter to President Wilson
6 October	Yugoslav declaration of independence
7 October	Polish declaration of independence
24 October	Battle of Vittorio Veneto
26 October	Resignation of Ludendorff
27 October	Kiel Mutiny
28 October	Czechoslovak declaration of independence
31 October	Turkish armistice
1 November	Hungarian declaration of independence
3 November	Austrian armistice
7 November	Revolution in Munich
9 November	Resignation of Prince Max in favour of Ebert
	Abdication of Kaiser
11 November	German armistice

1 Introduction

In December 1917 Maurice Hankey, Secretary to the British War Cabinet, recorded in his diary his appraisal of the difficulties facing the Allies:

> Russia practically out of the war; Italy very much under the weather after defeat; France unreliable; the USA not really ready; our own man-

power much exhausted by the senseless hammerings of the last three years; labour in a disgruntled state.[1]

On New Year's Eve Albrecht von Thaer, who was on the staff of Germany's High Command, wrote in his diary:

> Russia, this gigantic military power totally defeated, begs for peace; Romania the same. Serbia and Montenegro have simply disappeared.

He went on to pronounce Italy soundly beaten and France almost defeated, while U-boats continued to threaten Britain's overseas trade.[2]

Thus the same circumstances caused Hankey to be pessimistic and Thaer to be optimistic about their respective countries' chances of winning the war – though significantly the latter does not mention the home front. He did, however, go on to ask: 'Will America yet be able to turn the tide of history?' This chapter seeks to answer his question and to show how both men's feelings were belied by the events of 1918 – a year so momentous that Lyn Macdonald, who set out to give a complete eightieth anniversary account of it, found that she had written a whole book before she reached 5 April (*To the Last Man*, 1998). So this brief analysis cannot do full justice to the 'experience of men'; but it does attempt to convey the atmosphere of those desperate months.

2 Leaving and Entering the War

KEY ISSUE How much difference did the exit of Russia and the entry of America make to the outcome of the war?

a) The Treaty of Brest-Litovsk

In November 1917 Lenin, head of Russia's new Bolshevik government, issued his Decree on Peace calling on 'all belligerent peoples and governments to start immediate negotiations for a just and democratic peace ... without annexation and indemnities'. He then sent fellow-Bolshevik Leon Trotsky (along with representatives of Russian soldiers, sailors, workers and peasants) to attend peace negotiations with Germany and Austria at Brest-Litovsk. Both Lenin and Trotsky fully believed that the talks would soon be interrupted by the outbreak of revolution in Britain, France and Germany.

By January 1918 this hope had not been realised (though there had been strikes and food riots in those countries) and the Russian delegation was still refusing to accept peace terms so punitive that they shocked even some members of the German delegation. Russia was to give up Poland, Lithuania, the Ukraine and Finland, thus losing over a third of its population and more than half its agricultural and industrial resources. Trotsky refused to sign and Germany resumed its invasion of Russia in February. There was so little resistance that German troops advanced 150 miles in five days (thus achieving the lightning war planned for the Western Front in 1914). Lenin, whose priority was the survival of the Bolshevik government, convinced a bare majority of the Central Committee that the 'robber peace' must be accepted, his main argument being that it could be broken at the earliest opportunity.

The Treaty of Brest-Litovsk was finally signed on 3 March; as well as giving up the areas already demanded and its provinces on the Baltic Sea (all of which were put under German protection), Russia had to pay an indemnity of five billion gold roubles and to cease all Bolshevik propaganda. Thus Germany inflicted on its defeated enemy much harsher terms than it had later to accept at Versailles. Together with the Treaty of Bucharest (May 1918), which gave Germany control of Romania's wheat and oil supplies, Brest-Litovsk went a long way towards fulfilling the 1914 aim of German hegemony in central and eastern Europe (see page 17). The threat that Germany would realise the rest of its September Programme by inflicting a similar treaty on western Europe did much to stiffen the resistance of Russia's former allies, France and Britain.

As well as bringing territorial and economic benefits, the treaty did much to boost morale in Germany. It won strong support in the Reichstag, even from deputies who had voted for the 1917 Peace Resolution disavowing 'forced acquisitions of territory'. Above all, the cessation of war in the east allowed Ludendorff immediately to transfer troops and weapons to the Western Front by means of Germany's efficient railway system. Historians disagree about how many troops were transferred. Keegan refers to 50 'not indifferent' infantry divisions (over one and a half million soldiers).[3] Other historians stress that thousands of men deserted during the journey, where railway stations 'became the focus for political agitation and subversion',[4] and that 'Ludendorff's megalomania required that one million troops remain in Russia to enforce the peace and to exploit its resources'.[5] Certainly Germany now had enough troops on the Western Front to give Ludendorff the confidence to plan 'an annihilating blow before American aid can become effective'. At last Schlieffen's dream of a one-front war had been realised – though Germany's hard-pressed allies were still demanding help in Italy, Palestine and Salonika.

b) The Participation of America

Another transfer of troops was taking place across the Atlantic Ocean. An American officer describes the atmosphere on board the troop-ships:

My hill billies are having the time of their lives. They are packed in moderately thick, they are very adaptable and every new event is a new sensation, so by and large they are having one grand time.[6]

But a character in John Dos Passos's novel *Three Soldiers* (1921) revolts against conditions down in the stinking hold:

For how many days would they be kept in that dark pit? He suddenly felt angry. They had no right to treat a feller like that. He was a man, not a bale of hay to be bundled about as anybody liked. 'An' if we're torpedoed a fat chance we'll have down here', he said aloud.[7]

Both accounts are valid in so far as they convey the mixed feelings of young Americans, unready for the rigours of military life as they embarked enthusiastically on President Wilson's crusade for peace and freedom.

When Wilson had reluctantly declared war on Germany in April 1917 as a result of U-boat attacks on neutral shipping (see page 78), he justified America's entry into 'the most terrible and disastrous of all wars' in a speech to Congress:

1   The world must be made safe for democracy. Its peace must be planted upon the tested foundations of political liberty. We have no selfish ends to serve. We desire no conquest, no dominion. We seek no indemnities for ourselves, no material compensation for the sacrifices we shall
5   freely make. We are but one of the champions of the rights of mankind. We shall be satisfied when those rights have been made as secure as the faith and the freedom of nations can make them.[8]

The speech succeeded in its most immediate purposes: it was greeted with prolonged applause in Congress; young men flocked to join the forces; and American, British and French flags bedecked the streets of American cities. But Wilson's words sought subtly to distance his country from the imperialist ambitions of France and Britain, whom he always called 'associates' rather than allies. Accordingly, he told General John Pershing, US Commander-in-Chief, that 'the forces of the United States are a separate and distinct component of the combined forces, the identity of which must be preserved'. This aim was to be difficult to achieve in the 'bloody inferno' of the Western Front in 1918.

Even more problematical was to be the peacemaking role which Wilson claimed here and which he spelt out in January 1918 in his Fourteen Points. With their idealistic emphasis on democracy, national self-determination, open diplomacy and the prevention of future wars, they were not very welcome to his war-weary allies who expected some recompense for their long effort. There were some points of agreement, such as restoring independence to Belgium and Serbia and freeing Italians and Slavs from 'foreign domination'; the Allies even accepted the idea of a League of Nations. Although issues of potential disagreement were for the moment shelved, they were to cause dissension at the Peace Conferences of 1919 (see pages 121–124).

In April 1917 the might of America was more of a dream than a reality. Its Regular Army was small (only 130,000 men), ill-equipped and inexperienced in modern warfare. Not even the officers had much idea of what to expect, as is suggested by the advice given at Plattsburg training camp:

> Bring a pair of sneakers or slippers. They will add greatly to your comfort after a long march or a hard day's work. A complete bathing suit often comes in handy.[9]

The Air Force consisted of one squadron of antiquated planes. Only the Navy was able to participate immediately for America had already begun a huge ship-building programme; this was now accelerated and diverted into the construction of anti-submarine vessels and torpedoes to ensure the safe transport of their own and the Allies' troops and supplies. As the naval effort demonstrates, America's great advantage was its huge industrial capacity, which enabled it quickly to make good some of its deficiencies in military equipment. Also, of course, America had a huge reserve of potential recruits – though its black citizens were thought to lack military spirit and were welcomed only into Labour Corps.

By March 1918 31,000 semi-trained American troops had reached France safely, no transport ships having been torpedoed despite the fears of their occupants. Though eager (in the words of Private Sam Ross) 'to do our bit no matter how hard', the soldiers had to undergo further training in camps at some distance from the front line, where cafés, souvenir shops and brothels sprang up to cater for the needs of the Yankees or Doughboys as they were variously called. Later in their training they were attached to existing Allied units at the front but it was still Wilson's intention (despite pressure from the Allies) that the American Expeditionary Force (AEF) should not take part in battle until it was ready to form its own independent divisions – which would not be until 1919. But two days after the Germans launched their massive offensive on 21 March 1918 the British Ambassador urged the President to allow US troops already in France to serve in French and British divisions. Wilson authorised this as a temporary measure and (as the Ambassador's son wrote) 'in those few moments the scales had been finally weighted against the enemy'.[10]

Pershing, who considered that the Allies were 'done for', resisted even this temporary amalgamation of forces but he had to implement it. Sam Ross was able to write to his mother about his first experience in front-line trenches:

> We had only three men hurt and they had slight shrapnel wounds so you can see we were very lucky, as some of the other outfits were hit pretty hard. Claud and Quack were gassed. They are all right now. They got their masks on in time and the gas did not have much effect.[11]

This letter would have been subjected to Pershing's censorship (stricter than that enforced in any other army), which kept far-off American civilians ignorant of the miseries of trench warfare even when the AEF became involved in the costly defensive fighting of May and June. As will become clear, its troops fought with great determination and courage throughout that summer and autumn but, in the opinion of the chief historian at the US Army Center of Military History, 'the war ended before American commanders and staffs could attain full proficiency, adjusting their training methods and tactics to meet the demands of the Western Front'.[12] America's entry did not therefore give the Allies the means of gaining a quick victory over Germany.

The arrival of the AEF did, however, give a huge lift to the morale of weary French civilians and of Allied troops in France. Vera Brittain's reaction to her first sight of American soldiers typifies a widespread feeling of relief:

1 I pressed forward with the others to watch the United States physically entering the war, so god-like, so magnificent, so splendidly unimpaired in comparison with the tired, nerve-racked men of the British Army. So these were our deliverers at last, marching up the road to Camiers in
5 the spring sunshine! There seemed to be hundreds of them, and in the fearless swagger of their proud strength they looked a formidable bulwark against the peril looming from Amiens.[13]

By September Ludendorff had begun to sense 'looming defeat' in the face of 'the sheer number of Americans arriving daily at the front'.[14] It was to be this fear, rather than any decisive American action, which disastrously sapped German morale in the dark days of autumn.

3 Playing the Last Card: The Western Front

> **KEY ISSUE** Why did the Allies finally defeat Germany on the Western Front?

a) The Ludendorff Offensive: March–July

The Germans had not initiated an attack on the Western front since Verdun early in 1916; after their heavy losses in the battle of the Somme they concentrated instead on building up their defences (see page 37). This involved withdrawing their troops from 1,000 square miles of land, including various salients, and constructing the 'Hindenburg Line' of concrete blockhouses behind a series of fortified outposts and in front of an array of massive artillery. To impede enemy advance all the abandoned territory was laid waste: villages and towns were destroyed, crops burnt, minefields planted and wells poisoned.

At the same time, however, Germany waged its U-boat campaign and planned the land offensive which Ludendorff still believed to be the most effective means of making war. To this end he reorganised and re-equipped his divisions, dismounted a third of his cavalry and created special 'Storm Battalions' of troops trained to advance quickly ('like snakes over the ground') to infiltrate enemy lines of defence. These units were first used in the German counter-offensive at Cambrai in December 1917 (see page 47) and were now to be put to the test again in the big German attack planned for March 1918.

Ludendorff was optimistic: the collapse of the Russian and Italian armies in 1917 encouraged him to think that the same could happen to the French now that Germany's troops were concentrated on the Western Front. But it is not clear that his confidence was justified. While Keegan states that Germany had 'numerical superiority' (192 divisions to the Allies' 178), Chickering is equally emphatic that 'German active forces in the west numbered only about 80 per cent of the allied armies'. Both historians agree that Germany had less military equipment than the Allies at the beginning of 1918:[15]

	Germany	Allies
Machine guns (per infantry division)	324	1,084
Artillery	c.14,000	c.18,500
Aeroplanes	c.3,670	c.4,500
Trucks	23,000	c.100,000
Tanks	10	800

The main reason for these German deficiencies was the Allied blockade, which created shortages of crucial raw materials – even horses were a scarce commodity. Nevertheless, its superior training rendered the German army a well-oiled machine in itself. It was essential, High Command argued, to put it into action before more American troops could be sent across the Atlantic. This was the Germans' 'last card'.

All evidence testifies to Ludendorff's brilliant planning, carried out over two months of unremitting work. He intended to 'punch a hole' through the British lines, wanting to knock out first the enemy he most feared. For their part, the British were expecting an attack and were beginning to organise a 'defence in depth' similar to the Germans' own system. There were many who would have echoed the thoughts of Captain Jack Oughtred confided to his sweetheart on 13 March:

> The papers talk a great deal about the coming German offensive ... no doubt it's coming and in many ways a jolly good thing too, because we'll give those Bosche such a thin time as they've never had in their lives before.[16]

So effective was Ludendorff's deception, however, that the time and place of the attack took the British completely by surprise.

He chose to launch 'Operation Michael' along the 70 miles of the
Somme occupied by General Gough's 5th Army, which had been
depleted in numbers and morale at Passchendaele. The first day of
the attack (21 March) constituted 'the greatest concerted utterance
of modern industrialised warfare to that date'.[17] As well as artillery
and machine-gun fire and aerial bombardment, soldiers were subjected to attacks of lethal chlorine and phosgene gas. There were
38,000 British casualties that day (of whom 7,000 were killed and
21,000 taken prisoner) and in most places Gough was forced to
order retreat. It was the closest a British Army came to collapse in
the course of the war. Over the next two days the Germans advanced
12 miles capturing thousands more soldiers who, like Private Alfred
Grosch, were anxious to 'get out of this hell, as far back as possible'.[18] They seized Peronne, Bapaume and Albert and came close to
taking Amiens, from which they might have been able to reach the
Channel. No wonder church bells were ringing in Berlin on 23
March (see map).

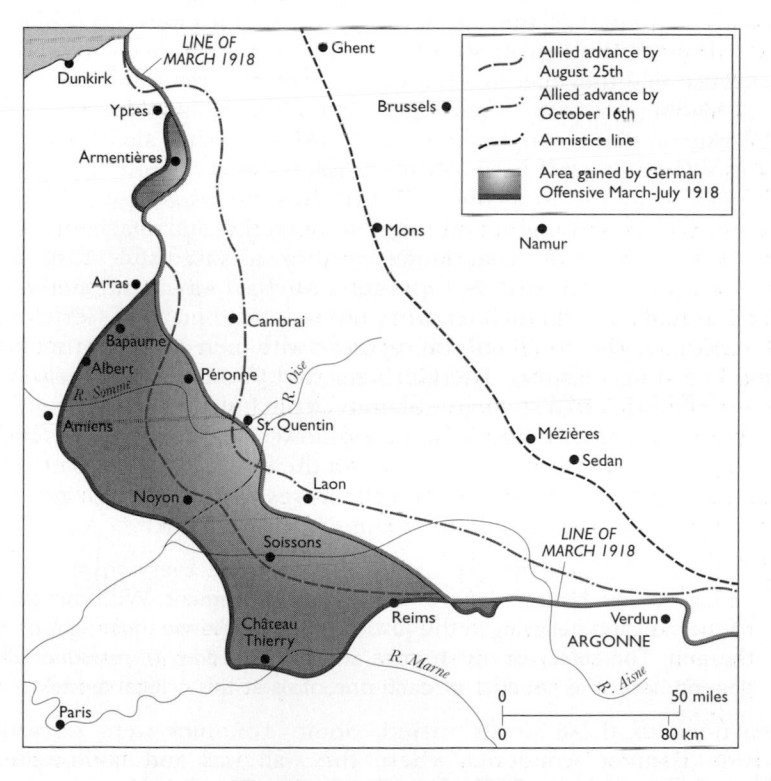

The Western Front in 1918.

If Ludendorff had now concentrated his forces on Amiens this operation might well have succeeded. Instead, the German Commander-in-Chief, described by Prince Rupprecht of Bavaria as 'a brilliant organizer but not a great strategist',[19] ordered the offensive to spread out in several different directions. The Allies, on the other hand, agreed at this point to unite their strategy under the direction of Field-Marshal Foch, the French Chief of Staff. His first order on 27 March was that the Allies 'must not retire a single inch'. Brave defensive actions followed, including one at Le Quesnoy described by an army chaplain:

i   Eventually the enemy got into one end of the village, and succeeded in knocking out our Lewis guns and their teams. Still this heroic band fought on, until at last only two or three rifles were left to crack. At 5 p.m. the two officers and nine men alone remained, and most of these
5   were wounded. In the gathering dusk this little company of eleven got away to the main body of troops behind, having held up the German Army in this sector for four precious hours! Who knows but that those four precious hours saved Amiens and perhaps the British Army itself![20]

By the beginning of April, however, the attacking troops were also reaching the end of their tether. Their casualties were even higher than those of the British and they suffered a self-inflicted wound in the sense that they had to advance through the area which Germany itself had laid waste in preparing the Hindenburg line. Moreover they had outrun their supply lines. It is not surprising that tired and hungry Germans fell prey to the temptations of abandoned British supplies of food and alcohol; 'entire divisions *totally* gorged themselves on food and liquor and failed to press the vital attack forward', complained Colonel von Thaer.[21] After a successful Australian counter-attack near Amiens, Operation Michael was abandoned on 5 April. It had gained much territory but sacrificed many of Germany's best soldiers, who could only be replaced with men released from hospital or young recruits. 'The Germans had purchased a tactical success at the price of a strategic calamity', concludes Trevor Wilson.[22]

A second surprise attack quickly followed on 9 April: Operation Georgette in the Ypres sector. It was on the third day of this battle, by which time Germany had gained the Ypres salient (though not the town itself), that Haig issued his famous Special Order:

i   There is no course open to us but to fight it out. Every position must be held to the last man: there must be no retirement. With our backs to the wall and believing in the justice of our cause we must fight on to the end. The safety of our homes and the Freedom of mankind alike
5   depend upon the conduct of each one of us at this critical moment.

Reactions to these words varied. Some Tommies were sarcastic; Private Baumer wondered where the wall was and commented: 'There is no doubt that things were serious but we didn't need anyone to tell us that'. But Vera Brittain found that it provoked 'a braver spirit in the hospital'.[23] This was certainly needed as men with 'frightful wounds' continued to pour into casualty clearing stations, where doctors like John Hayward could 'neither operate on nor evacuate cases fast enough to make much impression on the heaps'.[24] But there were similar scenes on the German side where over 100,000 soldiers lay dead, wounded or, in the case of some units, 'dead drunk'. By the end of the month this operation too had been abandoned.

The next German offensive (26 May on the River Aisne) was another masterpiece of tactical planning. It took German forces to within 56 miles of Paris – and thousands more Allied soldiers (including now many Americans) to prisoner-of-war camps, hospitals or cemeteries. But it petered out in early June amid problems similar to those which had dogged the Germans in the earlier attacks. This time they were hit by the first outbreak of Spanish flu, which affected nearly half a million German soldiers.

In the last massive attack, on the Marne in mid-July, the Germans found that the Allies were much more prepared (partly because the plans had been betrayed by German deserters). They had also to contend with American troops who were now arriving at a rate of 250,000 a month. Private Ross wrote proudly to his sister of the courageous action in this battle which led to his division being decorated. He added that:

> Some of the best and bravest fellows I have known are still along that river and on the top of that hill, but their names will never be forgotten, they are part of our history.[25]

This time German troops advanced only six miles before the Allies counter-attacked on 18 July, causing Ludendorff to call off both this and a further attack he had planned for Flanders; he also suffered a psychological collapse. Ludendorff must have known, though he did not yet admit, that his country's position was weaker as a result of his offensives despite their impressive territorial gains. For they had lengthened their line and created vulnerable salients at the same time as causing irreplaceable losses of men, equipment and horses. Keegan estimates that in six months the German Army had shrunk from 5.1 to 4.2 million.[26] Ludendorff had played his last card skilfully, arousing great alarm among and inflicting serious damage on his adversaries, but victory had eluded him.

b) The Allied Counter-Offensive: August–November

Much as they had suffered, the Allies had also gained advantages from the experiences of Spring 1918: an integrated command structure, stiffened morale (especially in the French Army) and a stimulus to greater professionalism. The last result is illustrated in the improved tactics adopted by the British Army, for which even Haig's critics give him credit. The most important innovations (some learnt from the enemy) were the element of surprise, better communications with greater use of radio, the large-scale use of tanks and their integration with artillery, infantry and airpower. Haig was also prepared to allow commanders greater use of their own initiative.

All these techniques were deployed in the Allied counter-offensive, spearheaded near Amiens on 8 August by the Canadians and Australians, on whom Haig relied greatly in this phase of the war. Sergeant Herbert Witherby describes

> tanks, infantry, cavalry, transport, all going forward, a wonderful sight. ... It was just such a day that in Western Canada puts the finishing touch to the ripening wheat.[27]

For Ludendorff, however, this was 'the blackest day of the German Army', not so much for the six miles of territory lost as for the 16,000 German prisoners taken by the likes of Sergeant Witherby who found them 'only too glad to get out of the battle'. Ludendorff blamed the defeat on the troops and ordered that deserters be summarily executed.

This same pattern was continued over the next month as the Allies repeatedly surprised the Germans by breaking off attacks and resuming them elsewhere. By 9 September they had retaken all the land lost in the spring offensives and unprecedented numbers of Germans continued to surrender, desert or feign sickness (plausible at a time when Spanish flu was still rampant). Because there is little available evidence of German soldiers' experience it is not easy to explain this drastic decline in German morale – even Niall Ferguson finds an explanation 'elusive', though he confidently dismisses any idea that men were weary of violence.[28] Clearly their earlier offensives had severely tested the endurance of German soldiers and placed them in extremely vulnerable positions, where they could not easily be supplied with food or protected by artillery. Disaffection could also have been spread by strike leaders from civilian life who had been punished by speedy conscription into the army (see page 88). Above all, the knowledge that Germany could not match the millions of new troops from America 'rotted the resolution of the ordinary German soldier to do his duty'.[29]

But in early September the German army had not collapsed and still occupied much of France: as one British soldier put it, 'Jerry was fighting a magnificent rearguard action'.[30] Thus even this offensive inflicted higher casualties among the attackers than among the defenders. Casualty rates rose still further when the Allies approached the Hindenburg line and other strong defence positions in late September. The AEF (now fighting as a separate Army) suffered heavy losses in the Argonne region near Verdun, as did the British and French in the Somme and the British and Belgians in Flanders. One of the most dangerous actions (29 September) was the crossing of the St. Quentin Canal, the banks of which were bristling with enemy machine-guns. Once across the canal the troops, as we see, were photographed receiving congratulations from senior officers.

British troops enjoy a brief moment of relaxation and celebration on the banks of the canal they have just captured.

It was on that same day that Ludendorff lost his nerve and announced to the Kaiser that the war was lost. On 3 October he wrote to President Wilson seeking what he hoped would be a mild armistice; but 16 October found him rejecting Wilson's unexpectedly tough conditions and ordering that 'the war must be continued with the utmost determination'. It was too late, as Hew Strachan points out:

> Having opened the door to peace, Ludendorff found he could not close it again. [People] could not recover their qualities of endurance once its continuation had been called into question.[31]

Now, rather than before Ludendorff's initial admission of defeat, the home front as well as the army began to collapse. On 26 October, refusing to recognise the true situation, Ludendorff threatened to resign if armistice negotiations were not broken off. To his astonishment the Kaiser accepted his offer (though not a similar one from Hindenburg). Ludendorff stormed out of the office and went into exile in Sweden.

Meanwhile Allied troops pushed the German armies back through northern France and southern Belgium (see the map on page 101), liberating occupied towns like Laon, where an emotional Mass of Thanksgiving was celebrated in the cathedral on 15 October. The knowledge that they had effectively won the war made it all the harder for soldiers (and their families) to accept casualties. A.B. Kenway describes how he felt in late October when his friend was killed by a shell just after they had set up some guns on the Messines Ridge:

> We knew the enemy was beaten; we knew it couldn't last much longer, and at this time, after three years in France and the end so near, Bob must be killed![32]

A more famous death at this last stage was that of Captain Wilfred Owen. He returned to the front after receiving treatment for shell-shock (see page 46) and took part in the battles of that autumn, receiving a Military Cross for his part in capturing a German machine-gun and, as he wrote to his mother, fighting 'like an angel'. On 4 November he was leading his men on planks and duckboards over a canal near the French border. His last words before being killed were, 'Well done! You are doing very well, my boy'. Among his papers were found his last poems, including 'Strange Meeting'; in this he dreams of meeting an enemy soldier he had killed, who tells him of 'The pity of war, the pity war distilled'.[33] Symbolic of the dead German of this poem is Paul Baumer, the hero of *All Quiet on the Western Front*:

> 1 He fell in October 1918, on a day that was so quiet and still on the whole front, that the army report confined itself to the single sentence: All Quiet on the Western Front. He had fallen forward and lay on the earth as though sleeping. Turning him over one saw that he could not
> 5 have suffered long; his face had an expression of calm, as though almost glad the end had come.[34]

When the German government finally accepted the Allies' peace terms in the early hours of 11 November, Owen's parents had still not received news of his death. The telegram arrived just as the church bells of Oswestry were ringing at 11 a.m. to announce the ceasefire.

They must have experienced the same poignant emotions as the friends and relatives mourning at the funeral of the French soldier-poet, Guillaume Apollinaire, who died of flu on 9 November while recovering from a serious head wound:

> The cortège was besieged by a crowd of noisy celebrants of the Armistice, men and women with arms waving, singing, dancing, kissing, shouting deliriously. ... Paris celebrating. Apollinaire lost. I was full of melancholy. It was absurd.[35]

German people, who were in the throes of revolution as well as defeat, had even more mixed and bitter feelings on 11 November. Many found it hard to accept that their country had been beaten for there had been no invasion. But, whatever political and military leaders might subsequently claim, there can be no doubt that Germany had been defeated on the Western Front. That defeat had been caused by plummeting morale in the face of Allied forces who outstripped Germany in men and in all types of military equipment, especially the tank which caused many German soldiers to panic. Haig's claim that it was 'in the great battles of 1916 and 1917 that we have to seek for the secret of our success in 1918' is still controversial. Some historians feel outrage at this defence of the 'butchery' of those years, while others agree that 'the cumulative effects of attrition' had played a critical part.[36] In any case, the desperate events and circumstances of 1918 are sufficient to account for Germany's defeat on the Western Front.

4 Explaining Defeat and Victory

> **KEY ISSUE** What was the most important reason for Germany's surrender?

A hard armistice was inflicted on the German delegation which met Marshal Foch in a railway carriage in the Forest of Compiègne near Paris. Germany was to evacuate within two weeks all captured territory including Alsace-Lorraine and give up the gains of Brest-Litovsk, to allow Allied troops to occupy the strategically important left bank of the Rhine, to surrender most of its navy as well as its artillery, machine-guns and aircraft, to return all prisoners-of-war and to make reparations for war damage. Until an actual peace treaty was signed the naval blockade was to continue. This section discusses the circumstances, apart from defeat on the Western Front, which lay behind this capitulation.

a) The Defeat of Germany's Allies

All the other Central Powers had surrendered before 11 November. The first to collapse was Bulgaria, which suffered heavy losses in the

Battle of Doiran launched by the Allies (now including Greece) from Salonika on 20 September. Although no British newspaper thought this attack important enough to merit a report, it caused Bulgaria to seek an armistice on 25 September after being told that Germany could do nothing to help.

At about the same time General Allenby advanced against the Turks in Palestine, finding – to his surprise – that his 'polyglot army' (which now contained West Indian and Nigerian contingents) fought with great valour. The Turkish Army was put to flight, allowing Allenby to enter Damascus on 1 October and sign peace terms at the end of the month. The fighting was over but malaria and Spanish flu now spread through the British Army, claiming the lives of four times as many Australians, for instance, as had the Turks.

Simultaneously the Austrian Empire had finally fallen apart, with the Yugoslavs, Poles, Czechoslovaks and Hungarians all declaring independence between 6 October and 1 November. This nationalist spirit was also displayed among the famished ranks of the Imperial Army – on a single day in early October there were 1,451 deserters from a largely Hungarian regiment. It was in these circumstances that Italy (supported now by substantial French and British reinforcements) launched an offensive on 24 October (to be known as the Battle of Vittorio Veneto). Whole Austrian divisions deserted to Italy which rapidly regained most of the land lost at Caporetto in 1917 (see page 65) as well as conquering some long-coveted territory in the Dolomites. When the Austrian government sought a ceasefire on 3 November, Germany stood alone.

The loss of its allies did not put Germany at a military disadvantage for it had been sustaining them throughout the war. But the collapse of what had seemed such a powerful alliance was a humiliating blow to its leaders and people. It can be no coincidence that Ludendorff decided Germany could not keep going on the very day that he heard of Bulgaria's decision to seek an armistice.

b) Revolution in Germany

On 29 September Ludendorff blamed Germany's misfortunes on the 'gentlemen' now being asked to form a ministry, who 'must now eat the soup they have ladled out to us'. This was the beginning the legend, later elaborated by Hindenburg and Adolf Hitler among others, that the army had been 'stabbed in the back' by civilian (principally Jewish) pacifists, socialists and strikers. Many believed this absurd story because the army had been allowed to retreat in good order and because the new civilian government (some of whose ministers were Jews) signed the armistice and later the Treaty of Versailles. The true story of political events is rather different.

Ludendorff and Hindenburg had themselves controlled Germany

since 1916, usurping even the Kaiser's authority. They had been responsible for all major decisions: the Hindenburg Programme, the submarine campaign, the Ludendorff Offensive. Opposition inside and outside the Reichstag was stifled, punished or ignored. It was Ludendorff who decided to ask for peace at the end of September, thus dealing the army (in Chickering's view) 'a stab from the front'.[37] At the same time he agreed to the formation of a new government which could be blamed for the defeat. The Kaiser appointed the liberal Prince Max of Baden as Chancellor and granted more power to the Reichstag. These concessions were not enough to quell the discontent generated by acute wartime hardship, the feeling that such sacrifice merited democratic rights and a sense of imminent defeat.

Revolution was triggered by the order given to the Navy on 27 October to do battle with Britain. Rather than give up their lives in vain, sailors at Kiel harbour extinguished the boilers on their vessels, refused to salute or obey officers, and abandoned ship to demonstrate in the town. Seaman Stumpf recorded that:

1   long years of accumulated injustice have been transformed into a dan-
    gerously explosive force which now erupts with great power all around.
    My God – why did we have to have such criminal conscienceless offi-
    cers? It was they who deprived us of all our love for the Fatherland, our
5   joy in our German existence, and our pride for our incomparable insti-
    tutions.[38]

Over the next few days crowds of Kiel citizens joined the sailors, demanding democratic government and an end to the war. Revolution spread to other towns, such as Munich, but there was little violence. Under pressure from President Wilson, as well as from the German people, Prince Max sent off the peace delegation to France on 9 November and resigned the Chancellorship in favour of Friedrich Ebert, leader of the main Socialist party (SPD) – who had lost two sons in the war. Amid continuing demonstrations the Kaiser was finally persuaded that only his abdication would save his country from civil war and Germany became a republic. 'I felt as if a heavy weight had suddenly been lifted from my heart', wrote Stumpf – but when he learnt that one of the conditions of the armistice was the surrender of the fleet, he gave way to despair:

I wish I had not been born a German. ... My Fatherland, my dear
Fatherland, what will happen to you now?[39]

These events demonstrate the close connection between the armed forces and civilians which existed in Germany, as in other countries participating in this total war. But they do not give any support to the idea that the former were betrayed by the latter.

c) Conclusion

'We cannot fight against the whole world', protested Ludendorff on 30 September. This feeling was induced by the weight of Allied troops on the Western Front, the continuing blockade and Germany's increasing isolation as its allies collapsed. There was a less obvious sense in which his despair was justified. Since 1914 the Allies had predominated over the Continental powers in industrial and financial resources (see Table on page 16), although this had not brought them victory in three and a half years of fighting. The entry of the United States in 1917 not only compensated for the loss of Russia – it gave the Allies an overwhelming advantage at a time when the German economy was weakened by the blockade and by the strain of supporting its industrially under-developed allies. Paul Kennedy's table below clearly demonstrates this imbalance.[40]

The US would be able to build enough ships, manufacture enough weapons, grow enough food and lend enough money to keep the Allies going for years – as long as their troops were prepared to go on fighting. The efficiency of Germany's army, railways and factories, the advantage of its central position and the patriotic endurance of its people allowed it to defy massive material odds for four years but in the end its economic disadvantage was decisive.

Thus a combination of factors caused Germany's defeat. Military reverses, inferiority in men and resources, civilian hardship, political unrest and trepidation about the economic weight of its enemies robbed a proud nation of its fighting spirit.

	UK/US/France	Germany/Austria-Hungary
Percentage of world manufacturing production (1913)	51.7	19.2
Energy consumption (1913), million metric tons of coal equivalent	798.8	236.4
Steel production (1913) in million tons	44.!	20.2
Total industrial potential (UK in 1900 = 100)	472.6	178.4

Industrial/Technological Comparisons with the United States but without Russia

References

1 M. Brown, *1918: Year of Victory* (Sidgwick & Jackson, 1998), p. 9.
2 Herwig, *First World War*, p. 351.
3 Keegan, *First World War*, p. 404.

4 Brown, *1918*, p. 36.
5 Herwig, *First World War*, p. 386.
6 Brown, *1918*, p. 148.
7 J. Dos Passos, *Three Soldiers* (Penguin, 1990), p. 38.
8 R. Hofstadter (ed), *Great Issues in American History* (Vintage Books, 1958), Vol. 2, pp. 216–17.
9 J. Cooke, 'The American Soldier in France' in Cecil & Liddle, *Armageddon*, p. 246.
10 Gilbert, *First World War*, p. 408.
11 Brown, *1918*, p. 152.
12 D. Trask, 'The Entry of the USA into the War and its Effects' in Strachan, *First World War*, p. 252.
13 Brittain, *Testament of Youth*, p. 298.
14 Keegan, *First World War*, p. 441.
15 Keegan, *First World War*, p. 421 & Chickering, *Imperial Germany*, pp. 178–9.
16 A. Wilkinson (ed), *Destiny: The War Letters of Captain Jack Oughtred M.C.* (Peter & Christopher Oughtred, 1996), p. 181.
17 Brown, *1918*, p. 48.
18 Lewis, *True Stories*, p. 212.
19 M. Kitchen, 'Ludendorff and Germany's Defeat' in Cecil & Liddle, *Armageddon*, p. 63.
20 Brown, *1918*, p. 69.
21 Herwig, *First World War*, p. 410.
22 T. Wilson, *The Myriad Faces of War* (Blackwell, 1986), p. 564.
23 Last three quotations from Brown, *1918*, pp. 96–9.
24 Lewis, *True Stories*, p. 258.
25 Brown, *1918*, p. 160.
26 Keegan, *First World War*, p. 439.
27 Brown, *1918*, p. 201.
28 Ferguson, *Pity of War*, pp. 387–94.
29 Keegan, *First World War*, p. 441.
30 Lewis, *True Stories*, p. 240.
31 H. Strachan, *The First World War* (Historical Association, 1994), p. 21.
32 Lewis, *True Stories*, p. 282.
33 E. Blunden (ed), *The Poems of Wilfred Owen* (Chatto & Windus, 1955), pp. 38–9 & 116.
34 Remarque, *All Quiet on the Western Front*, p. 320.
35 Blaise Cendrars quoted in Winter & Baggett, *The Great War*, pp. 317–19.
36 Laffin, *British and Bunglers*, p. 164 and T. Travers, 'The Allied Victories, 1918' in Strachan, *First World War*, p. 288.
37 Chickering, *Imperial Germany*, p. 191.
38 Horn (ed), *Private World*, p. 419.
39 *Ibid*, pp. 426 & 431.
40 Kennedy, *Great Powers*, p. 350.

Answering structured questions and essay questions on Chapter 6

Questions on the outcome of the war may now be tackled. This chapter will obviously be the most relevant but material will have to be drawn from Chapters 3, 4 and 5 to back up your arguments. Use the cross-references and the index to find what you need. It is also import-ant to consult some of the detailed histories and primary sources referred to in the footnotes and Guide to Further Reading.

1. Structured Questions

a) What economic factors contributed to the defeat of the Central Powers? (10 marks)

b) What political factors contributed to the defeat of the Central Powers? (10 marks)

c) Were either of these more important than military defeat in causing the collapse of the Central Powers in 1918? (20 marks)

a) Economic factors:
- The combined economic resources of the Entente countries were always much greater than those of the Central Powers.
- This advantage was further increased when America entered.
- Economic strength or weakness would affect production of war materials and food.
- The successful British blockade accentuated this imbalance.
- There can be no denying the importance of these factors in the long term but they could not actually win battles. After all, the Entente had not won the war by the summer of 1918. Some historians argue that German efficiency made up to some extent for inferior resources.

b) Political factors:
- Ludendorff blamed politicians for causing Germany's military collapse; but in fact political opposition did not get out of control until after his own admission of defeat.
- President Wilson claimed that the democratic Allies must prevail over the autocratic Central Powers; but this might well not have hap-pened. In any case the democracies suspended some civil and politi-cal rights during the war.
- Nationalism was a strong political force which contributed greatly to the collapse of Austria-Hungary.

c) Military Defeat:
- All the Central Powers were defeated militarily in 1918 – but some politicians and historians emphasise that Germany's army and terri-tory were still intact.
- Military action can only be resolved by defeat or victory.
- Nevertheless there is much to be said for Paul Kennedy's view that other factors were more important than military defeat. Thus the Austrian army was debilitated by nationalist unrest and the German army was weakened by lack of equipment (eg tanks) caused by economic weak-ness. In all Central Power armies hunger sapped fighting spirit.
- The outcome of the war was not, however, predetermined by any factors; much depended on the maintenance of morale, a factor which is not easily explained.

2. Essay Question

Why did the outcome of the war depend ultimately on breaking the stalemate on the Western Front?

This question makes two assumptions:
- The existence of stalemate on the Western Front, which should be explained (nature of weapons, trench warfare, rough equality of strength between the two sides, failure of attacks to break stalemate).
- The decisive nature of this as opposed to other war fronts. This is the more difficult part of the question. It could be dealt with by a series of points (+) and counter-arguments (−) with a conclusion at each stage (=):
+ Both sides had war aims here: Germany to dominate Belgium, France to get back Alsace-Lorraine, GB to secure Belgian neutrality.
− Both sides had aims elsewhere and Germany gained its eastern objectives early in 1918.
= The war continued because the aims in the west were so important to the countries concerned.
+ Germany actually occupied much territory here. Neither the occupied countries nor Britain were prepared to accept this.
− Germany occupied much Russian land and Russia simply had to accept its losses.
= Because there was a balance of strength in the west there was no alternative but for the two sides to fight it out.
+ Although Britain had naval supremacy this would not dislodge Germany from its dominant position on land.
− The blockade would starve German civilians into submission and make military resolution unnecessary.
= Blockade did weaken Germany but it would have taken too long for this method to have won the war on its own.

Conclusion: there are substantial reasons to support the contention that the war had to be resolved on the Western Front.

Source-based questions on Chapter 6

a) Read the extracts concerning American troop involvement on pages 97–99 (American officer, Dos Passos, Wilson, Plattsburg camp, Ross and Brittain). To what extent do these sources confirm Vera Brittain's impression of the Americans as 'our deliverers'? (10 marks)

b) Read the extracts on pages 100–106 concerning Allied troops in action during 1918 (Oughtred, the army chaplain, Haig, Ross, Witherby, Kenway and Owen). Look also at the picture on page 105. Do these sources support Haig's concept of fighting 'with our backs to the wall' or Owen's vision of 'the pity of war'? (10 marks)

Summary Diagram

The Changing Fortunes of Germany: 1918.

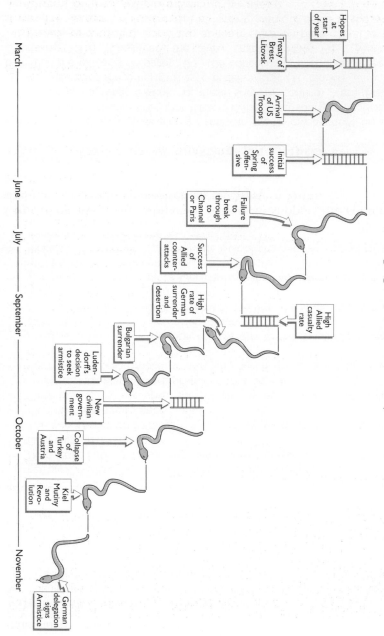

March —— June —— July —— September —— October —— November

Hopes at start of year

Treaty of Brest-Litovsk

Arrival of US Troops

Initial success of Spring offensive

Failure to break through to Channel or Paris

Success of Allied counter-attacks

High Allied casualty rate

High rate of German surrender and desertion

Bulgarian surrender

Luden-dorff's decision to seek armistice

New civilian government

Collapse of Turkey and Austria

Kiel Mutiny and Revolution

German delegation signs Armistice

7 International Legacies of the War

KEY DATES

1918 Civil War in Russia
1919 Treaties of Versailles, St Germain and Neuilly
Occupation of Fiume by d'Annunzio
Spartacist revolution in Germany
1920 Russo-Polish War
Treaties of Trianon and Sèvres
1921 Report of Reparations Committee
1922 War between Mustapha Kemal's forces and Greece
Mussolini's March on Rome
1923 Treaty of Lausanne
Occupation of Ruhr by French troops
Failed Nazi attempt to seize power in Munich
1926 General Strike in Britain
1929 The Great Crash
1931 Japanese invasion of Manchuria
1933 Appointment of Hitler as Chancellor of Germany
1934 German rearmament
1935 Italian invasion of Abyssinia
1936 German remilitarisation of the Rhineland
1938 Anschluss
Munich Agreement
1939 German occupation of Czechoslovakia
German invasion of Poland
Outbreak of Second World War

1 Introduction

The Great War brought forth a new world. It induced the birth of Communism and hastened the growth of nationalism – but both these ideologies engendered new conflict. A controversial Peace Settlement broke up the old European empires – but simultaneously increased the colonial possessions of the victorious countries. The United States emerged as a Great Power – but then retreated from the world it had helped to create. A new system of preserving peace arose from the ashes of destruction – but so too did militarist regimes. It was a mixed legacy.

2 Making a New World

> **KEY ISSUES** To what extent did the war bring about ideological change?

a) Old Empires and New Nations

1   The European War has brought about a crisis which may contain, as yet hidden within it, the moment for which the generations have been waiting. It remains to be seen whether, if the moment reveals itself, we shall have the sight to see and the courage to ... assert the independence of
5   our country.[1]

These were common sentiments among the frustrated subject peoples of Europe. They were expressed by Patrick Pearse, one of the leaders of Ireland's Easter Rising in 1916, the first of many nationalist revolts to spring from wartime circumstances. Despite its other commitments, the British Army had no difficulty in crushing the rising, which did not have widespread support. Indeed many Irishmen had volunteered for war service; thousands had fought bravely at Gallipoli and many more were to fight on the Somme and at Passchendaele, where a memorial was belatedly erected in 1998. The British government executed 16 of the rebel leaders, ignoring Pearse's warning that 'from the graves of patriot men and women spring living nations'. At the end of the war Sinn Fein (the nationalist party) set up an Irish Parliament and began guerrilla warfare against British troops, who were reinforced by a contingent of brutal ex-soldiers known as the Black and Tans. Civil war went on for four years, after which Lloyd George's compromise Treaty (creating the Irish Free State but keeping the six northern counties in the United Kingdom) was accepted by some but by no means all nationalists.

Meanwhile, the disintegration of the old Russian, Austrian and Turkish empires had revived nationalist hopes among their subject peoples. With encouragement from the western combatants (who supported nationalist revolts when they were directed against their enemies) they set up their own nation states which, like the Great Powers before 1914, coveted neighbouring territory. The subsequent struggles caused 'almost hopeless confusion' during the late stages of the war and in the months which followed the Armistice.[2] (See map, page 117.)

The first new nations were those which broke free in the wake of

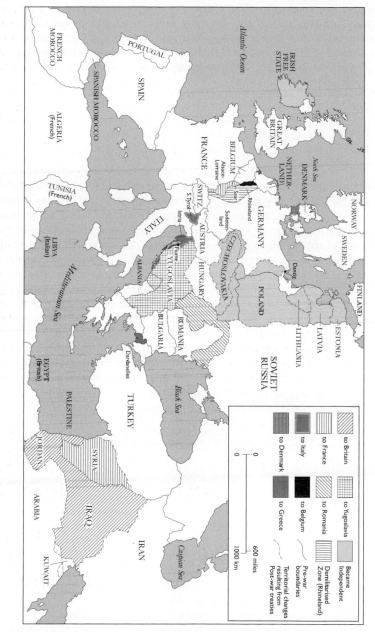

Territorial changes in Europe and the Middle East resulting from World War I.

the Russian Revolutions of 1917. Not all survived; by 1920 the Russian bear had clawed back the Ukraine, Georgia, Armenia and Central Asia. But the Baltic states of Finland, Estonia, Latvia and Lithuania, all of which received help from Germany, managed to cling on to their independence – at least until the next world war.

For Poland, partitioned between Russia, Austria and Germany since the 18th century, the Great War was the answer to an old prayer. With the defeat of their three oppressors nationalists were quick to establish the independent Polish state promised in President Wilson's Thirteenth Point. More contentious were the boundaries of the new country: those with Germany were long debated at Versailles; those with Russia were won as a result the Russo-Polish War of 1920–21; and those with Lithuania were not settled until the League of Nations sanctioned Poland's seizure of the former Lithuanian capital, Vilnius, in 1921.

Wilson's Tenth Point promised self-determination to the other peoples of Austria-Hungary, although this was well-nigh impossible given the mixture of national groups occupying the same land. A legion of Czech deserters, officially recognised by the Allies, formed the basis of an independence movement in Prague. By the end of October 1918 the new nation of Czechoslovakia already existed and was engaged in boundary wars with its neighbours, Poland and Hungary. It included the German-speaking area later known as Sudetenland (the subject of the notorious Munich agreement of 1938). Hungary too had formed a new democratic state at the end of October – but, as one half of the Dual Monarchy of Austria-Hungary, it received no encouragement from the Allies, who allowed Romania and Czechoslovakia to occupy more than half of its former territory. Also claiming freedom were the southern Slavs (or Yugoslavs). Whether or not they truly gained it is still a matter of bitter dispute: most of them were assimilated into the Greater Serbia so dreaded by Austria back in 1914 and so forceful in the Balkan region to this day. Nevertheless hopes were high in October 1918, when a Croatian nationalist proclaimed:

1 The old world is disintegrating, the loud clash of its collapse whips up our nerves into a new expectation which appears like a great light, like some new golden era which will bring happiness to all. And that future is all the more fascinating when it is compared with reality, with the
5 immediate wartime past of grief, poverty, the whole nightmare of war.[3]

Uncertain though their boundaries were, all the Slav nations which had formerly been part of the Habsburg and Ottoman Empires were now assured of their autonomy. More doubt surrounded the future of the other nationalities under Turkish rule, even though Wilson's Twelfth Point promised them 'an absolutely unmolested opportunity of autonomous development'. The persecuted Armenians proclaimed themselves independent in May 1918 but their bid for freedom did not survive the next two turbulent years. Arab hopes had received a setback with the 1917 Balfour Declaration naming Palestine as the national homeland of the Jews (see page 62) but Arab leaders still counted on the Peace Conference for the realisation of their dreams.

In fact it soon became clear that the concept of self-determination was not meant to apply to non-white people. France and Britain were more inclined to increase than to shed their imperial power after such a long and costly struggle and Wilson, for all his ideals, shared the racist attitudes common among Americans at that time. He refused, for instance, to discuss the future of Africa with the black American leader, W. E. B. Dubois, who sent him a memorandum in November 1918, suggesting that Africa be reconstructed 'in accordance with the wishes of the Negro race and the best interests of civilization'.[4] A similar petition on behalf of French-ruled South-East Asians came from the young Vietnamese nationalist, Ho Chi Minh, but it too was ignored. The Indian nationalist press declared after the Armistice that India's 'deeds and sacrifices justified her claim to an equality within the British Empire'.[5] This proved unacceptable to Britain: the Government of India Act of 1919 created an elected Legislative Assembly but this did not give Indians equality.

Self-determination proved to be a Pandora's box; once it was opened myriad nationalist desires flew out and created a havoc which the Great Powers could not control. A recent history of twentieth-century Europe concludes that 'The triumph of nationalism ... meant the rise of the minority as a contemporary political problem'.[6] That problem is still unresolved.

b) Revolution and Reaction

International stability was also threatened by the birth of a revolutionary new force. In Russia wartime conditions had helped to bring about the fall of the Tsar and the rise of the Bolsheviks in 1917 (see pages 56–57). By the time the Great War ended Lenin had established a Communist regime: land had been shared out among the peasants; class and titles had been abolished; banks and businesses had been nationalised; social insurance for all workers had been introduced. In theory power belonged to the 'workers, soldiers, peasants and all toilers'; in practice, a small group of Communist commissars ruled in their name.

Landowners, Tsarists and democrats resisted these radical changes and civil war swept the country. Russian soldiers returned from the front early in 1918 only to be recruited by the Bolshevik (Red) Army or by one of the counter-revolutionary (White) forces. Anxious both to stamp out Bolshevism and to bring Russia back into the war, the Allies (including Japan) sent troops and supplies to the Whites and imposed a naval blockade. The American businessman, Herbert Hoover, even used some of his personal fortune to distribute food and clothing to Russians (and other needy Europeans), believing that Bolshevism appealed only to hungry people. Nevertheless, the Whites had not prevailed by the time the Armistice came. After that western leaders found it difficult to justify the human and financial expense of continued involvement, although some like Churchill (now Minister for War) argued strongly that 'the foul baboonery of Bolshevism' must be destroyed.[7] All Allied troops left during 1919 except the Japanese who stayed on in eastern Siberia where they wanted to establish a sphere of influence. By 1920 the Red Army (under Trotsky's determined leadership) had defeated all the White forces – and Russia lay in a state of devastation and famine.

Meanwhile the ruling classes of many other countries feared that difficult post-war conditions and strenuous propaganda spread by the Communist International would cause the workers of the world to unite and seize power. Some governments employed excessively violent means to maintain control, using restive ex-soldiers to do their dirty work. Thus in Germany President Ebert used the *Freikorps* (right-wing groups of ex-combatants who felt betrayed by the peace) to put down an attempted Communist revolution by the Spartacists in January 1919. Over 1,000 people were killed or injured in the street fighting which resulted and after it was over the arrested Spartacist leaders, Karl Liebknecht and Rosa Luxemburg, were murdered. In May the *Freikorps* 'liberated' the German province of Bavaria which had been ruled by a revolutionary left-wing government since November 1918, shedding much blood in the process. In post-war Italy, too, the left and the right took violent action: workers agitated to be paid for days taken off at the Armistice; peasants returning from the front took over their landlords' estates; and black-shirted ex-soldiers threatened to march into lands which they considered to be Italy's just reward for its wartime sacrifice.

The fragile new regimes of central and eastern Europe felt especially vulnerable to the spread of Communism: for example, in 1919 a short-lived Soviet Republic was set up in Hungary. Even the well-established democracies, France and Britain, were uneasy. The French army was employed to keep a close watch on all Communist suspects and British troops were sent to police areas of left-wing union activity such as 'Red Clydeside', where workers were striking in favour of a 40-hour week.

As these two sections have shown, 'the First World War did not end tidily when the fighting ended on the Western Front in November 1918'.[8] Along the new frontiers of Europe and in the streets of its cities conflict dragged on as the world's statesmen gathered at Versailles in 1919. And they themselves contributed to the general disharmony by their exclusion of Bolshevik Russia from the peace-talks and by their stern attitude to the defeated powers.

3 Making Peace

KEY ISSUES How successful were the Allies in constructing a just
and lasting peace?

a) The Treaty of Versailles

According to the taped commentary given to visitors at Woodrow
Wilson's house in Washington, America's 'imperialist' allies at the
Peace Conference 'lost no chance of grabbing while the going was
good' and Wilson had to 'bargain away much that he held sacred'.
This is a crude over-simplification of the issues dividing the main
negotiators at Versailles. In fact the puritanical Wilson shared his
allies' desire to punish 'the wrong which Germany sought to do to the
world and to civilisation',[9] while at the same time wanting to implement his principles of democracy, self-determination, free and open
communication between nations and the prevention of war.

Clemenceau's purpose was certainly to strengthen France – but the
main point of this was to make any further German attack less likely.
It is true, too, that Lloyd George had imperialistic ambitions in the
Middle East – but he also wanted (as he made clear in the
Fontainebleau memorandum of March 1919) a just treaty which
would ensure the peace of Europe. Both these European leaders
claimed compensation from Germany, not least so that they could
repay the large war loans which America had no intention of can-
celling. Records of the conference show that all the leaders were prepared to compromise when necessary. From their long and anxious
deliberations emerged the much-criticised Treaty of Versailles.

The German government and people never regarded the Treaty as
anything other than a 'robber peace'. Soon British writers such as
J. M. Keynes and Harold Nicolson (both of whom had been at the
Conference) denounced it as excessively harsh and it became thor-
oughly discredited. Many historians have blamed it for causing such
bitter resentment in Germany that another war was almost inevitable.
'The road to World War II started here', claims one recent history,
using the words of Adolf Hitler to back up this view:

> What a use could be made of the Treaty of Versailles. ... How each one
> of the points of that Treaty could be branded in the minds and hearts
> of the German people until sixty million men and women find their
> souls aflame with a feeling of rage and shame.[10]

But other historians suggest that 'no allied peace would have been
acceptable to the Germans, who refused to face the reality of their
defeat'.[11]

The most obvious respect in which Germany suffered 'robbery' was
in losing 13 per cent of its pre-war territory. Alsace-Lorraine was

returned to France (without a plebiscite) in accordance with the primary French war aim. Clemenceau's desire to take the whole of the Rhineland was not, however, satisfied; in the end he settled for a temporary Allied occupation of the area followed by permanent demilitarisation. A compromise was also reached on Germany's rich Saar coalfield; France was allowed the products of its mines during a 15-year period of League of Nations administration, after which a plebiscite would decide whether the people wished to return to German rule – which they did. Plebiscites also determined that disputed border areas should be awarded to Belgium and Denmark. These western losses of territory were not excessively punitive.

More controversial were the adjustments to Germany's eastern frontiers. After long discussion 260 square miles of German land were awarded to the new state of Poland (some of it after a plebiscite), while the disputed city of Danzig was made into 'an autonomous state under the League of Nations'. Not only did this settlement separate East Prussia from the rest of Germany, it also turned many German-speaking people into Polish citizens. This was the territorial loss which most upset Germans, who regarded the Poles as an inferior race. At that time it seemed even more serious than the ban on Anschluss (the union of Germany with Austria) or the inclusion of three million Austrian Germans in Czech Sudetenland, both of which arrangements went against the principle of self-determination.

In addition Germany had to surrender its colonies on the pretext that it had shown itself unfit to govern subject races. Those in Asia were given to Japan, Australia and New Zealand as promised in 1914 (see page 20) and those in Africa to Britain, France, Belgium and South Africa. All were made mandates, which meant that the new governing countries were responsible to the League of Nations for 'the sacred trust of civilisation' – a 'nod in the Wilsonian direction'.[12]

Further severe blows to German strength, prosperity and pride were the permanent limitations placed on its armed forces and the high reparations payable to the Allies. To justify the latter a clause was inserted which caused enormous offence:

> Germany accepts the responsibility of Germany and her allies for causing all the loss and damage to which the Allied and Associated Governments and their nationals have been subjected as a consequence of the war imposed upon them by the aggression of Germany and her allies.

Sally Marks has suggested that clause 231 – often called the 'war-guilt clause' – was simply designed to 'lay a legal basis for reparations', that all the other defeated countries had to sign the same clause and that, arguably, Germany and its Allies did start the war (see pages 11–12). She claims too that the reparations, finally settled in 1921 at 132 billion gold marks, were not unreasonable in view of the reconstruction, war pensions and debt repayment they were supposed to cover.

It is evident that Germany could have paid a good deal more if she had chosen to do so, particularly since she paid little out of her own considerable resources. But Germany saw no reason to pay and from start to finish deemed reparations a gratuitous insult.[13]

Perhaps, however, it was the way in which the treaty was 'dictated' which insulted Germany most. German delegates were excluded from all discussions and then summoned 'like prisoners being brought in for sentence', a British diplomat remembers. Moreover the signing took place in the Hall of Mirrors at Versailles where the German nation had been proclaimed in 1871, thus conveying a feeling of French 'revenge for the injury done to her' in that year. He concluded that 'the necessary note of reconciliation, of hope, of a change of view, was entirely wanting'.[14] In the end, it is impossible to know whether a more lenient peace or more tactful treatment would have made defeat any more palatable to the German people. It is worth bearing in mind that Germany had inflicted an even harsher treaty on its defeated enemy at Brest-Litovsk (see page 96). It is also likely that, if Germany had won the war, it would have established the hegemony in Europe envisaged in the September Memorandum (see page 17).

b) The Treaties of St Germain, Trianon, Neuilly, Sèvres and Lausanne

The other defeated countries had to accept even heavier territorial losses; they also had to reduce their armies, to pay reparations and to admit responsibility for the war. The Treaty of St. Germain forced Austria to cede land to Italy, Czechoslovakia, Poland and Yugoslavia, mostly without plebiscites being held to determine what the inhabitants wanted. The new Austrian Republic had a population of only eight million and a very precarious economy. Hungary fared even worse; by the treaty of Trianon it lost over two thirds of its territory and nearly half of its population. In the Treaty of Neuilly Bulgaria was stripped of land, which went to Romania, Greece and Serbia. In none of these three treaties was self-determination the only principle invoked; when in doubt the peacemakers used land to reward those countries which had ended the war as victors.

One major beneficiary was Italy, which was awarded (without plebiscites) most of what had been promised in the Treaty of London in 1915 (see pages 22–23). It gained Trentino, South Tyrol, Istria and the port of Trieste, encompassing 1.6 million inhabitants, not all of whom were Italian. But, because the Dalmatian coast and the port of Fiume, which had been part of the original deal, were given to Yugoslavia and no African colonies were on offer, Orlando walked out of the conference and resigned. Right-wing groups exploited the situation to build up the myth of a 'mutilated victory' and in September

1919 nationalists led by d'Annunzio took matters into their own hands by marching into Fiume, which they occupied for over a year.

Another appeal to violence arose out of the Treaty of Sèvres, reluctantly signed by the Sultan of Turkey. It was a harsh settlement which not only took away Turkey's Arab lands but also gave control of southern Turkey to France and Italy, put the Dardanelles under an International Commission and gave much of Turkey's most useful territory to its old enemy, Greece. The treaty was challenged by Mustapha Kemal, the hero of Gallipoli (see pages 59–60). In 1922 he successfully led his rebel forces against the Greeks and also overthrew the Sultan, bringing yet another ancient empire to its end in the wake of the Great War. Reluctant to engage in further fighting Britain agreed to re-negotiate the Sèvres terms: by the Treaty of Lausanne (1923) the Greeks, French and Italians withdrew from southern Turkey and the straits were returned to Turkish control. Luckily for France and Britain, Kemal was not interested in regaining the Arab lands which they considered essential to their own economic and strategic interests: Syria, Iraq, Trans-Jordan and Palestine remained French and British mandates, to the acute disappointment of Arab leaders. Nevertheless, Lausanne was to prove the most enduring of all the peace treaties, perhaps because it was the only one to be negotiated rather than imposed.

The makers of all these treaties had been struggling to achieve varied and conflicting aims: the restoration and creation of independent nations; the reward and compensation of the victorious allies; the destruction of German militarism; and security for the future. Clearly the Versailles settlement was not perfect and some parts of it were hard to stomach. Indeed American senators found the new world role envisaged for their country so unpalatable that they refused to ratify the treaty, thus jeopardising it from the start. But to say that the Versailles negotiators made another world war inevitable is simply to exploit the benefit of hindsight.

c) The League of Nations

The most promising legacy of the war seemed to be the League of Nations, the international organisation designed by Woodrow Wilson to prevent future conflicts. The Covenant of the League was drawn up at Versailles and incorporated into all the treaties. Thus member countries promised to promote international peace:

1 By the acceptance of obligations not to resort to war;
   By the prescription of open, just and honourable relations between nations;
   By the firm establishment of the understanding of international law as
5 the actual rule of conduct among Governments:
   And by the maintenance of justice and a scrupulous respect for all treaty obligations in the dealings of organised peoples with one another.

These fine words undoubtedly reflected a widespread revulsion against war as a means of solving disputes – yet the League proved remarkably impotent and was unable to prevent the outbreak of another world war within a generation.

One major handicap from which the League suffered was the exclusion of the defeated countries. Lloyd George had asked in his Fontainebleau Memorandum:

> Why Germany, if she accepts the terms we consider just and fair, should not be admitted to the League of Nations, ... as she has established a stable and democratic Government. ... Might it not be safer that she should be inside the League than that she should be outside it?[15]

It was a good question – but for the time being the Central Powers were not deemed ready for membership. This meant that Germans especially saw the League as a victors' club and many remained suspicious even after they had been admitted in 1926.

Although it was a former ally, its new Communist regime made Russia still more of a pariah state. Despite Wilson's Fourth Point assuring Russia of 'a sincere welcome into the society of free nations under institutions of her own choosing' it was not allowed in until 1934. The most surprising absence was, however, that of the USA itself. In spite of Wilson's persuasive efforts, Congress decided to return to America's pre-war isolationism, thus breaking the President's heart and damaging the chance of world peace.

What the League lacked was the strength to enforce its decisions. The threat of trade sanctions against an offending country was empty without the weight of the world's economic giant behind it. Nor was the warning that force would ultimately be used credible since the League had no army of its own and enjoined on its members 'the reduction of national armaments'. In Britain and France 'a profound malaise' affected the armed forces in these war-weary years.[16] Falling government grants, poor pay and recruitment problems meant that they did not feel inclined to spare troops to enforce the League's Covenant. The French preferred to spend money on building its strongly defensive Maginot Line against the neighbour it still feared. And, of course, there would be no US army to step into the breach.

If distaste for war undermined the League's effectiveness belligerent feelings were by no means dead. While most soldiers returned to normal civilian life, some 'fighters who could not become de-brutalized' (to quote Hermann Göring's phrase) joined the German *Freikorps* or Benito Mussolini's *Fascio di Combattimento* (combat groups) in Italy. Both organisations were nourished by a cult of war which exalted violence. They were also fed by grievances arising from the peace treaties. Containing some hundreds of thousands, these groups were clearly a threat to democratic institutions. In Italy Mussolini used his squads to stage the so-called March on Rome in 1922, by which he persuaded the King to give him dictatorial power. Although Fascist Italy remained a member of the League of Nations Council its presence was increasingly threatening. In 1923 Mussolini sent troops back into Fiume, which had now been put under the League's control, and he used bullying tactics to get his own way in other crises during the 1920s.

Like Mussolini, Adolf Hitler had fought in the war and was enraged by its consequences. In the early 1920s he took over the leadership of the German Workers' Party (later known as the Nazi Party) and launched constant vitriolic attacks on those whom he saw as the culprits: the traitors, cowards, criminals and Jews who had brought about Germany's defeat; the English and French enemies who had inflicted 'the Peace of Shame'; the corrupt politicians and Jewish racketeers who were allowing Germany to go to rack and ruin. In a recent biography Ian Kershaw describes the war as a godsend for Hitler:

> Without the trauma of war, defeat and revolution, without the political radicalization of German society that this trauma brought about, the demagogue would have been without an audience for his raucous, hate-filled message.[17]

Hitler's brownshirted *Sturmabteilung* (stormtroopers), like Mussolini's Blackshirts, were used to destabilise democracy. Their leader, Captain Ernst Röhm, had suffered a severe facial wound early in the war, returned to the front and at Verdun received another serious injury which forced him out of the fighting. Devastated by the Armistice, he had joined the *Freikorps* and was a member of the German Workers' Party even before Hitler. His paramilitary connections enabled him to provide both weapons and manpower for the S.A. Even the once-mighty Ludendorff was attracted to the Nazi movement, lending his support to its disastrous attempt to seize power in 1923: the Munich Putsch. As this failure shows, defeat, loss and bitterness were not enough in themselves to bring about a Nazi regime. Most historians agree that, without the additional trauma of the Great Depression of 1929, Hitler might never have become German Chancellor in 1933. Once he had gained power, his ruthlessly aggressive nationalism, like that of Mussolini, was more than a match for well-meaning League of Nations delegates in their gleaming new headquarters at Geneva, who could pass resolutions only if *all* member countries agreed.

In fact the first serious challenge to the League's authority came not from either of these countries but from Japan, which, like Italy, was a permanent member of its ruling Council. Japan had actually done well out of the Treaty of Versailles – which is another reason for not giving that settlement too much responsibility for the breakdown of world order. Japan's only failure was in its bid to add an amendment to the League's Covenant giving 'all alien nationals of States members of the League equal and just treatment in every respect'. The rejection of this exemplary ideal can only be explained by the prejudices and fears of those countries which opposed it – principally Britain, Australia and America. When it was made clear to Wilson that the Japanese amendment would 'surely raise the race issue through-out the world', he vetoed it even though it gained a majority vote.[18]

This slight enraged the Japanese and discredited the League in their eyes. It cannot, however, be used as an explanation for their invasion of the Chinese province of Manchuria in 1931 because Japan's ambition for hegemony in the Far East predated the Great War and was sharpened by the ruinous effects of the Great Crash. The League's failure to inflict anything more than moral condemnation for this act of aggression against a member state was the beginning of its terminal decline. It failed to stop Italy's invasion of Abyssinia in 1935 and could not prevent any of Germany's infringements of the Treaty: rearmament (1934), conscription (1935), remilitarisation of the Rhineland (1936), Anschluss (1938), the occupation of Czechoslovakia (March 1939) and the invasion of Poland (September 1939). Militarism had proved a stronger force than conciliation.

Despite the clear links between the First World War and further conflict, it is too simple to claim, as did an 80th anniversary news-paper article, that 'World War II is a direct product of World War I'.[19] This chapter has suggested that some explosive factors pre-dated the war and that new unpredictable causes of conflict sprang up later. Nevertheless the article is correct to call this a 'terrible slaughter that changed the world', as Chapter 8 will further demonstrate.

References

1 Quoted in J. Finn & M. Lynch, *Ireland and England: 1789–1922* (Hodder & Stoughton, 1995), p. 92.
2 I. Geiss, 'Armistice in Eastern Europe and the Fatal Sequels' in H. Cecil & P. Liddle (eds), *At the Eleventh Hour* (Leo Cooper, 1998), p. 254.
3 M. Cornwell, 'Austria-Hungary' in *Ibid*, p, 293.
4 W. Keylor, *The Legacy of the Great War* (Houghton Mifflin, 1998), p. 226.
5 S. Bhattacharya, 'Anxious Celebrations' in Cecil & Liddle, *Eleventh Hour*, p. 195.
6 M. Mazower, *Dark Continent* (Allen Lane, 1998), p. 40.
7 Gilbert, *Churchill*, p. 410.
8 B. Bond, *War and Society in Europe, 1870–1970* (Fontana, 1984), p. 136.
9 D. Williamson, *War and Peace: International Relations 1914–45* (Hodder & Stoughton, 1994), p. 27. This book provides a more detailed treatment of the Treaties than can be given here.
10 Winter & Baggett, *Great War*, pp. 338 & 341.
11 Z. Steiner, 'The Peace Settlement' in Strachan, *First World War*, p. 303.
12 *Ibid*, p. 301.
13 S. Marks, 'The Myths of Reparations' in Keylor, *Legacy*, pp. 156–67.
14 Winter & Baggett, *Great War*, pp. 347–8.
15 Keylor, *Legacy*, p. 38.
16 Bond, *War and Society*, p. 140.
17 I. Kershaw, *Hitler, 1889–1936* (Allen Lane, 1998), pp. 73 & 87.
18 Keylor, *Legacy*, pp. 245–51.
19 Will Hutton in *The Observer*, 8 November 1998.

Summary Diagram
International Legacies of the War

Hopes	Dangers
Curbing of German militarism	Creation of German resentment
Principle of self-determination proclaimed	Preservation of old colonial empires
New nations created in Europe	Boundary conflicts between new nations and presence of minorities in unstable new states
Communist promise of social equality	Conflict between left and right
Compromise over some of victors' territorial claims	Defeated countries' resentment over loss of territory
Attempt to reward Italy for war efforts	Italian resentment that not all promises were kept
Negotiated Treaty of Lausanne	Dashing of Arab hopes for independence
Creation of League of Nations and arrangements to prevent future wars	Absence of defeated countries, Russia and USA from League
Widespread revulsion against war	Popularity of aggressive nationalism in Germany, Italy and Japan

8 Social, Economic and Cultural Legacies

Remember, as with the last chapter, that not everything that happened after the war was necessarily caused solely by it. As you read try to distinguish between adverse and beneficial effects and to decide which predominate. Finally, consider how the different themes explored here relate to people's actual lives.

KEY DATES

1915 Beginning of Dada movement
Publication of Brooke's poems
1916 Barbusse: *Under Fire*

1918 Franchise to British women over 30
Influenza epidemic
Housing Act (Britain)
Nash: *We Are Making a New World*

1919 Sexual Disqualification Act (Britain)
Vote to German women in Weimar Constitution
Sargent: *Gassed*
Publication of Owen's poetry

1920 Unemployment Insurance Act (Britain)
Jünger: *Storm of Steel*

1921 Famine in Russia
New Economic Policy (Russia)

1923 Hyper-inflation in Germany
Orpen: *To the Unknown Soldier in France*
Kipling: *The Irish Guards in the Great War*

1924 Dix: *War*

1925 Devaluation of the franc

1926 General Strike in Britain

1928 Franchise to all British women
Blunden: *Undertones of War*
Sherriff: *Journey's End*

1929 Graves: *Goodbye to All That*
Hemingway: *A Farewell to Arms*
Remarque: *All Quiet on the Western Front*
Aldington: *Death of a Hero*

1930 Sassoon: *Memoirs of an Infantry Officer*
Manning: *Her Privates We*

1932 Céline: *Journey to the End of the Night*

1 Introduction

The story of Leonard Thompson, a poor farm-worker from Suffolk, where people were 'literally worked to death', provides a good introduction to this complex topic:

> We were all delighted when the war broke out on August 4th. ... We were damned glad to have got off the farms.

After training, his regiment was sent to Gallipoli in 1915:

> 1 We all sat there – on the Hellespont – waiting for it to get light. The first thing we saw ... was a big marquee. It didn't make me think of the military but of the village fetes. Other people must have thought like this because I remember how we all rushed up to it, like
> 5 boys getting into a circus, and then found it all laced up. We unlaced it and rushed in. It was full of corpses. Dead Englishmen, lines and lines of them, and with their eyes open. We all stopped talking.

Thompson fought in the Gallipoli campaign, during which he saw much killing on both sides:

> 1 I shot through so many because I was a machine-gunner. Did they all die? – I don't know. You got very frightened of the murdering and you did sometimes think, 'What is all this about? What is it for?' But mostly you were thinking of how to stay alive. You felt brave and honoured
> 5 that you should be fighting for England.

He was then sent to France where he 'went through' the Somme, before being captured by the Germans at Arras in 1917, which he describes as 'the worst thing that ever happened' to him because of the near-starvation and ill-treatment he suffered. He was set free in November 1918 and returned home to an altered world.

> 1 The soldiers who got back to the village recovered very quickly. People who had lost their sons felt strange. Generally speaking, we were thankful that it was all over and we could get back to our work. Yet things *had* changed and people were different. The farm-workers who had
> 5 been soldiers were looked at in a new way. There were more privileges around than there used to be. ... We felt that there must be no slipping back to the bad old ways and about 1920 we formed a branch of the Agricultural Labourers' Union.

In 1921, however, there was a slump in agriculture:

> 1 The farmers became broke and frightened, so they took it out on us men. We reminded them that we had fought in the war, and they reminded us that they had too! So it was hate all round. Then we had to close down our Union Branch because nobody could afford to pay
> 5 the membership fee.

Thompson went on standing up for labourers' rights, even though 'it took a brave man to show his politics in Suffolk all through the 1930s', and eventually 'things changed'.

> I am old now. I read library books about the Great War – my war.[1]

In his laconic way Thompson tells us much about the varied legacies of war. We see first the shock he received from the grisly sight in the tent and wonder about how difficult he must have found it to talk about such experiences. We understand both his strong desire to return to normality and his sense that life ought to be better than it had been before. We realise that he questioned the war yet felt an enduring pride in what he had done for his country. It is clear that the war remained the most significant event in his life.

Many of the complex political, social and psychological effects of the war are illustrated in the experience of this one man. He felt the brutal tragedy of the war which is so much stressed by some historians, yet it lifted the scales from his eyes in the manner demonstrated by others. Leonard Thompson should help us to avoid oversimplifying the impact of his war.

2 Making Lands Fit for Heroes

> KEY ISSUE Did the war make people's lives worse or better?

a) Bereavement and Disability

As with all statistics about the Great War there are conflicting estimates of the number of combatants killed; but it seems clear that some nine million died, about one in eight of those who fought. Historians also disagree about whether it is right to refer to a 'lost generation'. Literally, this is a misnomer; but it seemed a fair description to groups (like Oxford and Cambridge colleges or communities from which Pals' Battalions had been recruited) which lost an unusually high proportion of their number. In New Zealand where 25 per cent of the eligible male population were casualties it felt as if 'almost a generation of the best men were wiped out'.[2]

All over the world there were people who had lost numerous loved ones. While serving as a VAD nurse Vera Brittain received news of the deaths of her fiancé, her brother and two other friends who had just left public school – but few today would sympathise with the fiancé's élitist lament a few months before he was killed that 'the same little piece of lead takes away as easily a brilliant life and one that is merely vegetation'.[3] Mrs Neale of Cookleigh lost three of her four sons: one of them had a daughter, Lucy, who never forgot the last walk she had with her 'kind and gentle' father as he went off to war.

> I can remember it now as if it was yesterday. I've never forgotten it, I never will, and that's been a lot of comfort to me many times in my life.[4]

Of the five Goodyear brothers who came over from Newfoundland only two survived. In France Madame de Grandière wrote that 'all the young men of our family had died and all my mother's friends were widowed, except one'.[5] In the light of this scale of suffering the debate over the term 'lost generation' seems rather academic.

Bereavement was almost universal. Winter claims that 'every family was in mourning', if not for a relative then for a friend or colleague.[6] The sudden death of friends caused lasting pain. At the age of 100, Florence Billington was still haunted by the loss of her boyfriend. After the war she met a spiritualist who could see a 'very young boy in khaki' standing behind her:

> On occasions since, I have felt his spirit visit me, that he was thinking of me and was somewhere near.

George Littlefair found it difficult to get over the death of a good pal, Joe Coates, who was killed beside him in the trenches. He found some consolation in 1997 when he visited Coates's grave in France:

> The last time I saw all the graves, they were little wooden crosses and now they are all nice white marble headstones and I thought what a big improvement. I was pleased.

As is shown in the pieces of oral history quoted above, mourners often found comfort in memories, in spiritualism and in visiting well-tended war cemeteries. Widows and orphans were aided, too, by state pensions, though these were not usually enough to live on.

In most countries pensions were also awarded to the ten million or so servicemen who had been left with permanent disabilities including the loss of limbs, blindness, lung damage, mental disorders and disfigurement. There was further compensation in the respect and help they often received from fellow-countrymen; being a wounded soldier 'counted for a lot' in the experience of Horace Gaffron, who lost a leg at the Battle of the Somme.[7] Perhaps the least appreciated group were the estimated 12 per cent whose faces had been smashed up by shellfire. The chances of surviving such horrific injuries improved during the war as a result of new techniques in plastic surgery. The Queen's Hospital at Sidcup, for instance, performed 11,000 operations between 1917 and 1922; much was done to rebuild men's faces but even so it was hard, wrote one nurse, 'to rekindle the desire to live' in men who knew that they would be appallingly disfigured.[8] Near the hospital there were special blue-painted benches which warned local residents that the occupants were likely to have hideous facial injuries. Families could not always accept these patients back and some of them committed suicide. Neither these nor the thousands of shell-shocked servicemen who killed themselves in the 20 years after the war are included in the official death toll or listed on war memorials.

It requires some effort to imagine these traumatic experiences, which are often most vividly conveyed in art and literature. For the people involved, the war clearly brought more pain than gain.

b) Standards of Living

It is harder to weigh up the benefits and losses in post-war standards of living and here, too, historians are divided. The losses are more immediately apparent. On all participant countries the war inflicted huge debts, inflation, disruption of trade, and destruction of homes, land and industrial resources. Every nation had to face the problems of demobilising millions of servicemen. For the Central Powers hunger caused by the continued Allied blockade added to the misery.

However, the greatest affliction of 1918–19 was the mysterious influenza virus which swept the world, accounting for far more deaths than the war itself – around 40 million. It affected alike prosperous and deprived areas, non-combatant and combatant countries, civilians and servicemen, fit and wounded. Its appearance at the end of the war made it harder to bear but there is no evidence that the two catastrophes were linked. In the middle of 1919 it began to disappear as mysteriously as it had arrived; deliverance from the consequences of war was to be both slower and more variable.

Russia was probably reduced to the worst condition of all. Already much affected by the Great War, Russian people had to bear the further strains of revolution, civil war, drought and rapid economic change. Industrial production declined drastically and in 1921 five million people died of famine. Yet even here some recovery was possible. Under the New Economic Policy Lenin made some concessions to capitalism and by 1926 production figures of food, coal and steel were creeping up to pre-war levels.

There were miserable conditions also in central European countries, especially those which had been defeated. In Bulgaria, for example, famine was only prevented by emergency imports from America. During the early 1920s the influx of nearly half a million refugees from troubled neighbouring countries placed such a burden on Bulgaria's resources that the League of Nations had to come to the rescue with a loan in 1926. These instances of international benevolence did not console the Bulgarians, who blamed their sufferings on the losses inflicted by the Treaty of Neuilly (see page 123).

Especially difficult to assess is the situation of Germany where, too, the post-war settlement was held responsible for all economic ills. But even after losing 13 per cent of its territory Germany was much stronger than its former allies and stood more chance of returning to normality. The new democratic regime (known as the Weimar Republic) did much to ease the process of demobilisation by providing emergency work projects, housing subsidies, dole for the unemployed and, most expensively of all, pensions for those disabled, widowed and orphaned by the war. Not surprisingly, perhaps, such spending was given a higher priority than the payment of reparations. It helped to keep unemployment within bounds in the 1920s – but it created rapid inflation which robbed many people (notably the disabled veterans) of any potential benefits. It is easy now to judge German politicians for their lack of fiscal foresight or even to suggest, as Ferguson does, that 'it would have been better if Germany had had a more authoritarian government ten years earlier'.[9] In fact, after reaching a crisis in 1923, the German economy began to improve: the introduction of a new currency ended hyper-inflation and American loans under the Dawes Plan enabled reparations to be paid more easily. The Weimar Republic might well have survived had it not been assailed by extreme forces from right and left and thrown into disarray by the Great Crash.

For France the economic priority was to repair the ten departments which had been devastated by German occupation and looting. Remarkably, this task was accomplished within seven years. In the expectation that reparations would be paid, the French government financed the reconstruction out of borrowing, thus saddling itself with an even higher national debt and accelerating inflation. The French occupation of the Germany's industrial Ruhr area (1923), in reprisal for the non-payment of reparations, not only wrought havoc with the German economy but also proved an expensive venture for France. In 1925 Poincaré brought inflation under control by devaluing the franc. This restored confidence and made French exports very competitive so that industrial production increased. By the later 1920s most French people had a higher standard of living than they had enjoyed before the war.

Britain's situation was similar to that of France. In both countries standards of health and welfare had risen during the war, which had stimulated measures to improve the care of children, the soldiers of the future. By the end of the war British infant mortality rates had fallen to the lowest level ever, whereas as late as 1915 it had been 'more dangerous to be a baby than a soldier'.[10] At the same time trade unions had ensured that the wages of workers, on whom the government depended so heavily for uninterrupted production, had doubled – and not all of this rise was eroded by inflation. It is true that both increased state involvement and the stronger position of organised labour were trends begun in Edwardian times, not entirely attributable to what Arthur Marwick calls 'the deluge' of war.[11] But there is no doubt that the war led to better living standards.

At the end of the war Lloyd George's coalition, which sought re-election, made its famous promise to create a land 'fit for heroes', hoping to satisfy the new aspirations of soldiers like Leonard Thompson. At the same time Britain, which had borne the brunt of financing the Allies, faced a war debt of over £11,000 million and a greatly disrupted export trade. Thus not all reconstruction promises were kept, though there were significant reforms. The Housing Act of 1918 subsidised the building of over 200,000 houses between 1919 and 1921 and the Unemployment Insurance Acts of 1920 and 1921 increased benefits for unemployed workers and their families – though agricultural labourers were excluded from the scheme. Such social policies continued even after the 'Geddes Axe' cut government spending in 1921. By that time the post-war boom was over and unemployment had risen to almost two million. Trade Union power declined and wages fell during the 1920s, as Leonard Thompson and his Union colleagues found. In 1926 a cut in miners' wages gave rise to the General Strike. Even eight years after the Armistice it was still the war which workers invoked. In the words of one Labour MP:

> The men who fought from 1914 to 1918 are quite as ready to put their backs to the wall in opposition to those who want to force wages down, as they were to fight the Germans. Threaten us with what you like.[12]

The Conservative Government took up the challenge and some of its members treated the General Strike as another war. After only nine days the government's special newspaper (edited by Winston Churchill) was able to announce that the Prime Minister in Downing Street had received the strikers' 'surrender'. Times remained hard for many working people but 'the absolute destitution which had haunted the poor of Edwardian Britain was banished' in the wake of the war.[13]

It is difficult to generalise about post-war standards of living. From country to country, from class to class, from family to family, from year to year, economic conditions varied. This variation has caused historians to take a pessimistic or an optimistic view according to the angle from which they view the matter. There is, however, general agreement that economic recovery from this long and costly war got under way with surprising speed.

c) Women and Families

> Demobbed [from the Women's Royal Army Corps], I went home. There they wanted to treat me as a sort of heroine. ... They praised me for all the wrong things. When I tried to tell them what the War had taught me, they were hurt in their turn.

The feelings of Mrs A.B. Baker, which are similar to those of many men returning home from the front, tell us something of what women gained and lost from the Great War. She was praised for her patriotic contribution to the war effort but in reality her experience was more complicated. She had been sickened by the sight of 'half a company of men blown to pieces by bombs' at Etaples; she had translated letters from French parents whose daughters had been made pregnant by English soldiers; she had given sexual comfort to a terrified young sergeant; she had visited a Quaker boyfriend who was in prison as a conscientious objector; she had met German prisoners and realised that they were just 'friendly men'; and she had prayed for the war to stop and 'set all us poor prisoners free'.[14] Thinking for herself was her real gain, as it was for many other sheltered young women in Europe.

Thousands of women left home to live in hostels near the factories where they were needed to produce war goods; some served near the front line in nursing corps or in the women's armed services; most earned higher wages than ever before performing jobs normally thought unsuitable for women. In doing all this they were less protected and more independent than most women had hitherto been. Of course the work was often hard, unpleasant and dangerous. In addition women employees frequently faced criticism or even abuse from male colleagues, who feared for their own jobs and wage rates, and from the general public who feared for women's virtue. In Britain, for instance, the Ministry of Munitions trained and paid older women to 'act as guardians', befriending 'foolish girls' and warning any who behaved unsuitably.[15] Married women had additional worries and responsibilities in wartime, especially in countries where there were desperate shortages. For women in Vienna, queueing, scrounging and hunting for food and fuel, the war did not bring much freedom, especially as elderly fathers or young sons took charge where possible; it was felt in this patriarchal society that 'there must be a man in the family in times like that'.[16] To women as to men the war brought grief, anxiety and danger mixed with a measure of pride and opportunity. But did women, as has often been suggested, win from the war permanent improvements in their economic, social and political status? Modern historians are not so sure that they did.

In France, Theodore Zeldin suggests, the war 'did not make all that much difference to the women'.[17] A higher proportion (40 per cent) than elsewhere in Europe had already been working outside the home. This figure increased during the war and in 1917 women led the way in striking for better pay and conditions. Afterwards, however, women's employment declined and husbands who returned from the front could still by law expect obedience from their wives. Furthermore women in France, where there had been no widespread suffrage movement, did not gain the right to vote until 1944. Whether most of them were unhappy with their lot it is hard to judge.

German women responded patriotically to the extreme demands the war placed on their country. They worked hard to feed their families and also to keep industry and agriculture going – the female workforce increased by 46 per cent. Few questioned the Demobilisation Committee's demand that women should give up their positions to returning soldiers and 'devote themselves to their former duties of taking care of the home and having children'. But many women did show independence in refusing to return to paid domestic service, often preferring to remain unemployed. Such assertiveness, claims Richard Bessel, aroused fears among men 'whose roles had been severely challenged by the war' – especially as German women had gained equal voting rights in 1919. Bessel goes on to argue that politics remained a 'male realm' because of the dominance of the 'front generation', which was responsible for bringing to power the 'militantly anti-feminist' Nazi Party.[18] He does not mention that large numbers of women voted for Hitler.

The experience of British women during and after the war was similar to that of German women. In their case, too, recent historians find that their war service did them little good. Deborah Thom states that:

> War had not challenged the sexual division of labour or the notion of the male bread-winner. These roles were only suspended for the duration and then only in some households.[19]

It is true that the gains of 1918–19 – the franchise for women over 30 and the removal of restrictions on women entering the professions – benefited respectable middle-class women rather than, say, the young female munitions workers to whom the government professed to be so grateful. Thus Asquith was being somewhat disingenuous in asking 'How could we have carried on the War without them?' as he announced to Parliament that he had changed his mind on female suffrage.[20] Arguably, too, even these concessions would not have been made had it not been for women's pre-war campaigning and progress. But it is a mistake to be too dismissive about women's gains, for all women had the vote within ten years and 'women's attitudes and aspirations had changed in the direction of increased self-confidence and willingness to stand up for themselves'.[21]

All over Europe the most obvious sign of change was in the appearance of women: they looked different in the shorter skirts and bobbed hairstyles which had proved so much more practical in factories, at the front and on the farm. There was a new code of behaviour to go with the new look; the chaperone had been an early casualty of the war and it was now acceptable for a young woman to go out to the cinema or dance-hall with a boyfriend or with girlfriends. It is hard to say how far these new habits explain the rises in illegitimacy and divorce which occurred in most countries during and after the war. Much moral concern was expressed about the trends – even though marriage was also on the increase. Most people, men as well as women, were only too happy to take up family life again after the upheavals of war.

3 Depicting the War

KEY ISSUES How and why has the depiction of the First World
War in art and literature varied?

This section illustrates the role played by art and literature in colour-
ing our impressions of the war. It cannot do justice to such a rich
topic but students can explore it further by looking at the paintings
in the Imperial War Museum and similar collections abroad and reading the works of literature mentioned in the footnotes and bibliography.

a) Art and the War

Like so many other people, artists welcomed the war. When Otto Dix
joined the German Army, for instance, he hoped that it would give
him 'tremendous experiences inaccessible in civilian life'.[22] The
Canadian Wyndham Lewis urged fellow artists that they could not
'afford to miss that experience.'[23] Since the early 20th century was a
time of experimental (*avant-garde*) work in the arts, the war was seen
as a new challenge. For Futurist artists, who aimed to break with the
past and to celebrate modern technology, dynamism and power, conflict would be 'a violent incentive', wrote Christopher Nevinson. And
for those artists who explored apocalyptic themes, prophesying
upheaval and calamity, the war was a kind of fulfilment.

Many artists volunteered, often joining special Artists' Units. Their
skills were in great demand for a range of tasks, such as making
models for target practice, constructing masks for soldiers with facial
injuries, creating camouflage – or even painting signs for the latrines.
Later some were appointed official war artists with the more general
duty of depicting the battlefield. Always they worked under the severe
constraints imposed by trench life and the censorship imposed by
governments.

Moved by the slaughter they had witnessed, many artists felt com-
pelled to convey their experiences in uncompromising terms. They
undertook a mission to modify the heroic view of war shown in pro-
pagandist posters, advertisements and newspaper prints. Nevinson
abandoned his triumphalist view of war but still used abstract
Futuristic forms in paintings like *French Troops Resting* (1916), in which
a group of exhausted soldiers take advantage of a few moments'
respite by the side of a road (see page 139). General Sir Ian Hamilton,
the Gallipoli commander, wrote a preface to the catalogue for the
1916 exhibition of Nevinson's works which, he said, would bring the
soldier 'closer to the heart of his own experiences than his own eyes
could have carried him'.[24] The exhibition was well attended and all
the paintings sold. Later Nevinson abandoned Futurism altogether;

French troops resting, 1916. by C.R.W. Nevinson.

he became an official war artist but the Department of Information rejected his naturalistic painting, ironically entitled *Paths of Glory*, because it showed dead bodies lying in a trench. When Nevinson displayed it with a notice saying CENSORED pasted across it, he was reprimanded by the Home Office.

Even though most of the official British war artists did not toe the government line they were allowed to go on working. Paul Nash arrived on the Western Front in 1917 and witnessed the aftermath of the Battle of Passchendaele – 'the most frightful nightmare'. In 1918 he wrote to his wife:

I It is unspeakable, godless, hopeless. I am no longer an artist interested
   and curious. I am a messenger who will bring back word from the men
   who are fighting to those who want the war to go on forever. Feeble,
   inarticulate will be my message, but it will have a bitter truth, and may
5 it burn in their lousy souls.

Soon after this Nash produced one of the most famous paintings of the war, *We Are Making a New World* (1918) (see page 140). This battlefield landscape contains no soldiers: but the mounds of mud resemble helmets rising from the ground; the blasted tree stumps represent human remains; and the red clouds symbolise blood. This, together with other 'funny pictures' by Nash, was passed by the censor, Colonel Lee, because it could not 'give the enemy any information'.[25] It does not seem to have

Gassed, by John Singer Sargent.

We are making a new world, by Paul Nash.

worried the Department of Information that Nash was conveying such a hostile impression of the war. Another artist commissioned by the government, the fashionable American portrait-painter John Singer Sargent, produced an equally unforgettable image with his realistic depiction of soldiers blinded by mustard gas: *Gassed* (see page 140). It was shown at the Royal Academy in 1919 and hailed as picture of the year.

Even more popular were the late war paintings of Irish artist, William Orpen. Originally commissioned to paint the Peace Conference, Orpen duly recorded the scene in *The Signing of the Peace Treaty in the Hall of Mirrors*, which was well received. But Orpen 'kept thinking of the soldiers who remained in France for ever' and expressed this idea by using the same ornate background of the Hall of Mirrors for another commissioned work, *To the Unknown Soldier in France*. Beside a flag-draped coffin stood two young soldiers, naked apart from their helmets, over whom hovered two cherubs. This painting was a great success in the Royal Academy show of 1923 but the Imperial War Museum (which had commissioned it) found it unacceptable. It can be seen in the museum today but the soldiers have been painted out. Nevertheless, Orpen and his fellow-artists had produced enough revealing work to ensure that the men who fought and died between 1914 and 1918 would be immortalised in their fashion. They had helped to shape a new perception of war. Meanwhile the troops themselves preferred the more traditional heroic or humorous view of themselves as depicted in the cigarette cards and picture postcards which so many of them collected during the war (see below).

A TRIBUTE TO THE INFANTRY.

A TRIBUTE TO THE CAVALRY.

On the other side of No-Man's Land Otto Dix also struggled to communicate his view of the slaughter. The semi-abstract *Signal Flare* (1916) is a shocking scene of dead soldiers entangled in barbed wire (see front cover). Dix was unable to forget his experiences after the war and used sketches he had brought back from the front to produce a series of 50 gruesomely realistic etchings entitled *War* (1924). One of them shows worms crawling out of a skull; and if Dix's obsession with death's capacity to sustain life seems too sensational it should be compared to the matter-of-fact memory recorded by a British war veteran:

1 I was told to go back into what had been No-Man's Land and bury the
    old dead of the Newfoundland Regiment. ... They looked very ragged,
    very ragged and the rats were running out of their chests. The rats
    were getting out of the rain, of course, because the cloth over the rib
5   cage made quite a nice nest and when you touched a body the rats just
    poured out of the front.[26]

Dix also painted many mutilated ex-soldiers, who symbolised his revulsion from war. His work was never popular in Germany and was to incur the wrath of the Nazis, who banned him from exhibiting in 1934 and burned some of his paintings.

The war, therefore, stimulated in soldier-artists not so much new styles of art as an intense effort to express the truth. Artists not directly involved in the fighting reacted in other ways. The ageing Claude Monet, a close friend of the French Prime Minister Clemenceau, painted water-lilies as the 'only way to avoid thinking about what is happening' – though this was difficult since his son was at the front and wounded soldiers constantly passed by his house at Giverny. After the war he gave a series of these peaceful, consoling paintings to the nation. A very different response was that of the Dada movement, founded by Tristan Tzara in Switzerland in 1915. Feeling that the war had 'institutionalized absurdity' and killed individuality itself, the Dadaists depicted only the illogical and the ridiculous – 'a harlequinade made of nothingness'. The most authentic contemporary artists, they claimed, were the field commanders who 'painted in blood'. Dadaism did not last long but it helped to give rise to the 'warped imaginings' of the post-war Surrealist movement.[27]

b) The War in Literature

Many ordinary soldiers also did sketches of trench life and the battlefield – but there were many more who wrote about their experiences. Poetry was quite widely read – many a knapsack contained a comforting slim volume – and the war inspired many to try their own hand at verse. Some 2,225 British war poets have been identified. Similarly, the war encouraged prose and 400 novels by ex-servicemen were published in Britain alone. These works were devoured by other veterans, like Leonard Thompson, who had an insatiable desire to read about the war. It would be interesting to know which of the two main kinds of books he preferred – the romantic or the disenchanted.

Britain's favourite romantic war-poet was Rupert Brooke, whose *1914 and Other Poems* (1915) sold very well in its year of publication and was reprinted 28 times by 1920. Educated at Rugby and Cambridge, Brooke was already an established poet before 1914; he joined up eagerly but never took part in battle as he died of blood poisoning on the way to Gallipoli in 1915. In poems like 'The Dead' he expresses the patriotic mood felt by so many at this stage in the war; he urges bugles to blow out over 'the rich Dead':

1   These laid the world away; poured out the red
    Sweet wine of youth; gave up the years to be
      Of work and joy, and that unhoped serene,
      That men call age; and those who would have been,
5   Their sons, they gave, their immortality.[28]

There is evidence that front-line soldiers, anxious civilians and bereaved relatives found solace in such words. In Ernest Raymond's best-selling post-war novel, *Tell England* (1924), three public-school boys join up at the age of 18 and when one of them is killed their Colonel quotes Brooke's lines to his friends. All three eventually die and the army padre (a character based on Raymond himself) survives to 'tell England' of the 'beauty' of their sacrifice.[29] This is typical of the romantic view presented in most war literature published during and soon after the war. It tended to use an exalted vocabulary – words like 'honour', 'valour', 'sacrifice' – which disguised reality; Brooke's 'sweet, red wine of youth' does not conjure up the same image as 'young men's blood'.

In Germany an even more heroic spirit prevailed, which is typified by Ernst Jünger. He served in all but the first two months of the war and received special training as a stormtrooper – as well as 14 wounds. His account of these experiences in *Storm of Steel* (1920) vividly conveys the excitement and fulfilment to be found in battle (see the quotation on page 42). His warrior is 'a new kind of man, a new species, destined to rule'.[30] From the community of such comrades a new and better Germany would grow, prophesied such writers as Jünger. This was a theme which Hitler was able to exploit for his own purposes.

Mussolini had the same opportunity in Italy where war was celebrated even more passionately. The poet Gabriele d'Annunzio engaged in daring exploits in all three services, even though he was over 50. 'I owe the highest and purest conquests of my spirit to the bloody and muddy war,' he wrote. After the Armistice he longed for 'a heroic reason to go on living'; he found it in 1919 when he led the invasion of Fiume (see page 124), where 'our war completes itself, crowns itself'.[31] For the writer Filippo Marinetti, founder of the Futurist movement, the uniforms, machinery, sounds and smells of war were beautiful; he fought in the First World War and later in

Italy's Abyssinian campaign, which he regarded as 'the finest futuristic poem which has yet appeared'.[32]

On the other hand, writers disillusioned with war tried to communicate its often horrifying reality. They described everyday incidents instead of conjuring up high-flown themes. They drew attention to pain rather than excitement and conveyed futility rather than glory. One of many examples is Wilfred Gibson's 'Breakfast' (1917):

1 We ate our breakfast lying on our backs
   Because the shells were screeching overhead.
   I bet a rasher to a loaf of bread
   That Hull United would beat Halifax
5 When Jimmy Stainthorpe played full-back instead
   Of Billy Bradford. Ginger raised his head
   And cursed, and took a bet, and dropt back dead.[33]

From the pens of Sassoon, Owen and Rosenberg (see pages 106 and 44), Wilhelm Klemm and Alfred Lichtenstein, Benjamin Perét and Guillaume Apollinaire flowed verse in the same sardonic vein. Apollinaire, for instance, seemed to be 'laughing at the risks' with his word pictures written in forms which reflect the subject matter – a coffin, a bursting shell, sheets of rain. Not all this work emerged during the war, when censorship rules applied; in fact it is amazing that Barbusse's outspoken novel, *Under Fire*, was published in both France and Britain in 1916 (see pages 39–40). Only four of Owen's poems had appeared before he was killed and the first collection was not published until 1919. This contained his own preface which sums up his approach and that of many other soldier-poets:

1 This book is not about heroes. English poetry is not yet fit to speak of
   them. Nor is it about deeds, or lands, nor anything about glory, honour,
   might, majesty, dominion, or power, except War. Above all I am not
   concerned with Poetry. My subject is War, and the pity of War. The
5 poetry is in the pity.[34]

Like the art exhibitions of this time, this volume had a mixed reception. Some critics hailed Owen as the greatest poet of the war; others condemned these 'shell-shocked' verses.

Ten years after the Armistice the controversy about the disenchanted as opposed to the idealistic depiction of the war was intensified when a host of works by ex-servicemen showed the war in a far from favourable light. From Britain came Edmund Blunden's memoir *Undertones of War* (1928), R. C. Sherriff's play *Journey's End* (1928), Richard Aldington's novel *Death of a Hero* (1929), Graves's memoir *Goodbye to All That* (1929), Sassoon's *Memoirs of an Infantry Officer* (1930), Frederic Manning's novel *Her Privates We* (1930) and a new volume of Owen's poetry with an introduction by Blunden; from Germany came Remarque's *All Quiet on the Western Front* (1929); from America came Hemingway's *A Farewell to Arms* (1929); and from

France came Louis-Ferdinand Céline's *Journey to the End of the Night* (1932). All these works (especially *All Quiet on the Western Front*) were widely read at the time, as they have been ever since, undoubtedly shaping our perceptions of the war. They have often been blamed for creating an anti-war myth and fuelling pacifism (see pages 40 and 41).

One charge is that these writers give an unduly depressing view of war service. In fact, all their books tell of the comradeship, the sense of duty, the stoicism, the food, drink and cigarettes, the recreation, the jokes, the beauties of nature which helped to keep soldiers going. Even Sassoon, who had lost his faith in the war by 1917, remembers feeling cheerful on the evening before the Battle of Arras:

1   Having seen the men settled into their chilly barns and sheds, I stuffed myself with coffee and eggs and betook myself to a tree stump in the peaceful park of a white chateau close to the village. .... The sun was just above the tree-tops; a few small deer were grazing; a rook flapped
5   overhead; and some thrushes and blackbirds were singing in the brown undergrowth. Nothing was near to remind me of the War; only the enormous thudding on the horizon and an aeroplane humming across the clear sky. For some obscure reason I felt confident and serene. My thoughts assured me that I wouldn't go back to England tomorrow if I
10 were offered an improbable choice between that and the battle.[35]

The close similarity between this passage and Sassoon's diary entry for that day (7 April 1917)[36] suggests an answer to another criticism: that these post-war reminiscences lack authenticity. Of course they should not be read as documentaries, but all were based on the first-hand experience of men who had served at the front. It had taken them ten years or so to publish because, says Aldington, it was 'a question of trying to communicate the incommunicable'.[37] As well as the happier moments, they contain some terrible stories and images, more upsetting than anything a soldier would write in a letter to his family. Aldington's hero George Winterbourne walks over a captured area in 1918:

1   The ground was a desert of shell-holes and torn rusty wire, and everywhere lay skeletons in steel helmets, still clothed in the rags of sodden khaki or field grey. Here a fleshless hand still clutched a broken rusty rifle; there a gaping, decaying boot showed the thin, knotty foot-bones.
5   He came on a skeleton violently dismembered by a shell explosion; the skull was split open and the teeth lay scattered on the bare chalk; the force of the explosion had driven coins and a metal pencil right into the hip-bones and femurs. In a concrete pill-box three German skeletons lay across their machine-gun with its silent nozzle still pointing at
10 the loop-hole. They had been attacked from the rear with phosphorous grenades, which burn their way into the flesh, and for which there is no possible remedy. A shrunken leather strap still held a battered wrist-watch on a fleshless wrist-bone. Alone in the white curling mist, drifting slowly past like wraiths of the slain, with the far-off thunder of

15 drum-fire beating the air, Winterbourne stood in frozen silence and contemplated the achievements of civilized men.[38]

Such accounts are no more harrowing, however, than the unsensational memories recorded in recent years by war veterans (see, for example, pages 130 and 142). The sum of other evidence suggests that Paul Fussell was right in claiming that 'the war was much worse than any description of it in the 1920s or 1930s'.[39]

Nevertheless, critics claim, these middle-class writers (most of whom were junior officers) give 'a highly subjective, unbalanced and misleading version' of front conditions. They reacted more strongly than working-class soldiers against trenches where, writes one historian, the amenities were no worse than those of an average 'slum yard'.[40] Let Leonard Thompson reply: he came from a family of ten living in a brick-floored cottage with no running water within a mile but in the trenches of Gallipoli, he writes, 'we wept, not because we were frightened but because we were so dirty'.[41]

Needless to say, memoirs and novels do not tell us the whole truth about the war. They do not tell us about international diplomacy or political manoeuvres or military strategy because their authors had no experience of these matters. But the literary work of the men of every nation, class and rank who fought in the war forms an important part of our evidence, valid in its own terms. It should be read by anyone who wants to gain some idea of what it felt like to fight in almost unimaginable conditions. For, as Ezra Pound graphically put it, they knew what it was to have been 'eye-deep in hell'.

c) Conclusion: Remembering the War

All forms of art, says Peter Conrad, were affected by the war which 'brutally and irrevocably modernized mankind'.[42] Civilians were no less conscious of it than servicemen. The composer Edward Elgar, whose pre-war music had been filled with optimistic, patriotic themes, wrote his sorrowful Cello Concerto in 1919 to express his sense of loss. The war was assimilated into post-war Modernist writing like that of D.H. Lawrence, T.S. Eliot, Ezra Pound and Virginia Woolf. Its lingering presence is summed up vividly by Woolf's Mrs Dalloway; when news of the suicide of a shell-shocked young man is brought to her while she is entertaining, she thinks: 'In the middle of my party, here's death.'[43]

Another who was left with an abiding sense of death was Britain's bereaved imperialist poet, Rudyard Kipling, one of whose Epitaphs of War introduced this book (see page 1). For several years after the war Kipling worked with others to provide suitable cemeteries and memorials for those who had been killed. Travellers today can observe the fruits of such labours all over Europe, where the tiniest villages commemorate those who were slain and whole towns, such as Ypres in Belgium which was completely rebuilt in the 1920s, are sites of memory in themselves. From the autoroutes of northern France motorists can see huge battlefield monuments like those at Thiepval and Vimy Ridge, as well as innumerable war cemeteries. Mountain walkers or skiers might come across the grim war memorial on Monte Grappa in the Italian Dolomites or Brancusi's fine commemorative sculptures at Tirgu-Jui in the Romanian Carpathians. From a cruise-boat on the eastern Mediterranean passengers could glimpse the coastal graveyards and memorials on the Gallipoli peninsula in Turkey. Over eighty years after the end of the war new names and graves are still being added as more soldiers' remains are found and the sites continue to be visited by descendants, tourists and students.

Kipling also undertook the task and the duty of writing a history of the part played in the war by the Irish Guards, his dead son's regiment. It took him five years of research, using official records, diaries and interviews with surviving members of the regiment, to create this monument to service and sacrifice. Like much imaginative literature about the war, Kipling's fine history (published in 1923) conveys a wide variety of experience and emotion. It ranges from personal anguish over the heavy losses of the Somme to regimental pride about a creditable parade put on for an inspection by the King of the Belgians. Kipling is filled with wonder at 'what armed mankind faced in the trenches in those years'. He marvels 'that, while they lived that life, it seemed to them sane and normal, and they met it with even temper and cool heads'. At the end of the book he expresses his own mixed feelings, as well as those of the men themselves, as they disbanded in Spring 1919:

1 They had been a 'happy' Battalion throughout, and ... one that had 'done as well as any' in a war that had made mere glory ridiculous. Of all these things nothing but the memory would remain. And, as they moved – little more than a Company strong – in the wake of their sen-
5 iors, one saw, here and there among the wounded in civil kit, young men with eyes which did not match their age, shaken beyond speech or tears by the splendour and the grief of that memory.[44]

This present book has tried to evoke both the splendid courage and the terrible grief brought forth by the First World War.

References

1 R. Blythe, *Akenfield: Portrait of an English Village* (Allen Lane, 1969), pp. 38–44.
2 C. Pugsley, 'New Zealand: The Heroes Lie in France' in Cecil & Liddle, *Eleventh Hour*, p. 208.
3 Roland Leighton to Vera in A. Bishop & M. Bostridge (eds), *Letters From a Lost Generation* (Abacus, 1999), p. 111.
4 R. Van Emden & S. Humphries, *Veterans* (Leo Cooper, 1998), p. 207.
5 Cecil & Liddle, *Eleventh Hour*, p. 102.
6 J. Winter, *Sites of Memory, Sites of Mourning* (CUP, 1995), p. 2.

7 The last three experiences are recorded in Van Emden & Humphries, *Veterans*, pp. 129, 132, 148.
8 A. Bamji, 'Facial Injury: The Patient's Experience' in Cecil & Liddle, *Armageddon*, p. 499.
9 Ferguson, *Pity of War*, p. 432.
10 The Bishop of London quoted in R. Pope, *War and Society in Britain, 1899–1948* (Longman, 1991), p. 63.
11 A. Marwick, *The Deluge: British Society and the First World War* (MacMillan, 2nd edn 1991), p. 49.
12 S. Hynes, *A War Imagined: The First World War and English Culture* (Bodley Head, 1990), p. 409.
13 J. Lawrence, 'The First World War and its Aftermath' in P. Johnson (ed), *20th Century Britain* (Longman, 1994), p. 167.
14 Lewis, *True Stories*, pp. 380–6.
15 C. Haste, *Rules of Desire* (Chatto & Windus, 1992), pp. 33–5.
16 R.J. Sieder, 'Behind the Lines' in Wall & Winter, *Upheaval of War*, p. 116.
17 T. Zeldin, *France 1848–1945: Ambition and Love* (OUP, 1979), p. 350.
18 R. Bessel, *Germany after the First World War* (OUP, 1993), pp. 239 & 272.
19 D. Thom, 'Women and Work in Wartime Britain' in Wall & Winter, *Upheaval of War*, p. 317.
20 Quoted in P. Bartley, *Votes for Women 1860–1928* (Hodder & Stoughton, 1998) p. 97. This *Access in Depth* volume discusses the issue in more detail than is possible here.
21 Marwick, *The Deluge*, p. 31.
22 J. Winter, 'Painting Armageddon' in Cecil & Liddle, *Armageddon*, p. 860.
23 P. Gough, 'The Experience of British Artists in the Great War' in *Ibid*, p. 848.
24 R. Cork, *A Bitter Truth: Avant-Garde Art and the Great War* (Yale UP, 1994), p. 132.
25 *Ibid*, pp. 198–202.
26 Van Emden & Humphries, *Veterans*, p. 130.
27 P. Conrad, *Modern Times, Modern Places* (Thames & Hudson, 1998), pp. 209–11.
28 Gardner, *Up the Line to Death*, p. 48.
29 E. Raymond, *Tell England* (Cassell, 40th edn 1973), p. 177.
30 Obituary of Ernst Jünger, who died in 1998 at the age of 102, in *The Times*, 19 February 1998.
31 A. Bonadeo, *D'Annunzio and the Great War* (Associated University Presses, 1995), pp. 126–8.
32 Conrad, *Modern Times*, p. 211.
33 Gardner, *Up the Line to Death*, p. 84.
34 J. Glover & J. Silkin, *First World War Prose* (Penguin, 1989), p. 389.
35 S. Sassoon, *The Complete Memoirs of George Sherston* (Faber & Faber, 1972 edn), p. 420.
36 Sassoon, *Diaries*, p. 150.
37 Hynes, *A War Imagined*, p. 424.
38 R. Aldington, *Death of a Hero* (World Distributors Ltd, 1965), p. 367.
39 P. Fussell, *The Great War and Modern Memory* (OUP, 1977), p. 174.
40 C. Barnet, *The Collapse of British Power* (Alan Sutton, 1984 edn), pp. 429–31.
41 Blythe, *Akenfield*, p. 40.
42 Conrad, *Modern Times*, p. 203.

43 V. Woolf, *Mrs Dalloway* (Penguin, 1925), 201.
44 R. Kipling, *The Irish Guards in the Great War: The Second Battalion* (Spellmount, 1997), pp. 78 & 193.

Summary Diagram
Social, Economic and Cultural Legacies

Losses	Gains
9 million dead servicemen – grief for families and friends	Recognition and comfort provided by war memorials and war cemeteries Improved techniques in surgery mean more survive
Permanent disability of 10 million survivors	Financial help for veterans Greater state involvement in people's welfare – higher standard of living (Fr, GB)
Hunger in blockaded countries	
Inflation robs benefits of their value	
High war debts	
Devastation of fighting areas	Beginnings of recovery by 1920 in most countries
Women lose wartime jobs	Women gain vote in some countries
Rise in illegitimacy and divorce rates	Greater freedom for single young women
Deadlier weapons for use in future wars	Technological advance (e.g. tanks, aeroplanes, gas)
Loss of pre-war innocence and patriotism	More realistic attitude to war

150 Social, Economic and Cultural Legacies

Answering essay questions on Chapter 8

With more research, using books mentioned in the footnotes or recommended in the bibliography, this chapter could serve as a starting point for comparative or thematic questions on the social and economic effects of the war. E.g.:

Assess the social and economic gains and losses resulting from the First World War.

The summary diagram could help with this question, examples and illustrations being drawn from the chapter and from further reading.

Factors to bear in mind during the discussion include:

* neither gains nor losses were uniform or universal
* these categories (gain and loss, social and economic) over-simplify reality
* some post-war trends may not be due entirely to the war

In your conclusion you should decide whether you see the war more as a useless slaughter or as a beneficial influence.

Further Reading

As the last participants die off, interest in the First World War shows no sign of abating, with new books appearing every year. The 80th anniversary years of the 1990s were especially productive.

1 General Histories of the War (in order of publication)

A.J.P. Taylor, *The First World War* (Hamish Hamilton, 1963) – although over 30 years old, this is still one of the most stimulating general histories, well-written in Taylor's characteristic ironic tone and full of excellent illustrations.

John Laffin, *Butchers and Bunglers of World War One* (Alan Sutton, 1988) – as its title implies, this book is unsparing in its criticism of the generals and their tactics.

Philip Haythornthwaite, *The First World War Source Book* (Arms and Armour, 1992) – not a collection of primary sources but an indispensable compendium of information about all aspects of the war.

Hew Strachan, *The First World War* (Historical Association, 1994) – a fair and succinct account by an acknowledged expert.

Martin Gilbert, *The First World War* (Weidenfeld & Nicolson, 1994) – this long, chronological account provides no analysis but through the accumulation of detail leaves a lasting impression of the war.

Jay Winter and Blaine Baggett, *The Great War* (Penguin, 1996) – written to accompany an excellent BBC television series, this compassionate history concentrates on how the war affected ordinary men and women.

Hugh Cecil & Peter Liddle (eds), *Facing Armageddon: The First World War Experienced* (Pen & Sword, 1996) – inspired by the 1994 80th anniversary international conference at Leeds, this volume of over 60 articles aims to challenge 'the distortions of popular mythology'. It contains many fresh insights.

Holger Herwig, *The First World War: Germany and Austria-Hungary* (Arnold, 1997).

Roger Chickering, *Imperial Germany and the Great War* (CUP, 1998) – this book and Herwig's provide a new emphasis for English-language readers on the war from the other side of the trenches. Both deal with the experience of troops and civilians as well as high-level strategy.

John Keegan, *The First World War* (Hutchinson, 1998) – a clear and readable history of the fighting by one of the best military historians, who reveals disastrous miscalculations without attacking everything that the generals did. He manages to view the war from above and from below.

Hew Strachan (ed), *The Oxford Illustrated History of the First World War* (OUP, 1998) – this extremely useful volume contains essays on all the important aspects of the war as well as some very striking illustrations.

Niall Ferguson, *The Pity of War* (Allen Lane, 1998) – by posing a series of questions to which he often gives surprising answers, Ferguson certainly makes his readers think afresh about the war.

2 The Western Front

Malcolm Brown, *The Imperial War Museum Book of the Western Front* (Sidgwick & Jackson, 1993).
John Keegan, *The Face of Battle* (Jonathan Cape, 1976).
Alistair Horne, *Verdun 1916: The Price of Glory* (Penguin, 1993 edn.).
John Laffin, *A Western Front Companion* (Alan Sutton, 1994).
Leon Wolff, *In Flanders Fields* (Pan, 1961) – a vivid narrative of Passchendaele.

3 Other Aspects of the War

James Joll, *The Origins of the First World War* (Longman, 1984).
Keith Wilson (ed), *Decisions for War* (UCL Press, 1995)
Peter Liddle, *The Sailors' War* (Blandford Press, 1985).
Nigel Steel & Peter Hart, *Defeat at Gallipoli* (Macmillan, 1994).
Norman Stone *The Eastern Front 1914–1917* (Hodder & Stoughton, 1975).
Orlando Figes, *A People's Tragedy* (Jonathan Cape, 1996).
Martin Clark, *Modern Italy, 1871–1982* (Longman, 1984).
Peter Kilduff, *Richthofen: Beyond the Life of the Red Baron* (Arms & Armour, 1993).
Malcolm Brown, *1918: Year of Victory* (Sidgwick & Jackson, 1998).
Gerard De Groot, *Douglas Haig* (Unwin Hyman, 1988) – a fair biography of a controversial figure.

4 Impact of War

J.-J. Becker, *The Great War and the French People* (Berg, 1985).
H. Cecil & P. Liddle, *At the Eleventh Hour* (Leo Cooper, 1998) – shows how the end of the war was greeted over the world.
Richard Cork, *A Bitter Truth: Avant-Garde Art and the Great War* (Yale, 1994) – an international survey of war art.
Paul Fussell, *The Great War and Modern Memory* (OUP, 1975).
Samuel Hynes, *A War Imagined* (Bodley Head, 1990) – this book and the last one focus on British culture.
Arthur Marwick, *The Deluge: British Society and the First World War* (Macmillan, 1991 edn.) – controversial but interesting.
David Williamson, *War and Peace: International Relations 1914–45* (Hodder & Stoughton, 1994) – the war in its international context.

Jay Winter & Richard Wall, *The Upheaval of War* (CUP, 1988) – deals with the involvement of civilians in many countries.

5 Experience of War

This has been a fruitful field of research in recent years.
The following collections of personal experiences are especially vivid:
Malcolm Brown, *The Imperial War Museum Book of the First World War* (Sidgwick & Jackson, 1991).
Richard Van Emden & Steve Humphreys, *Veterans: The Last Survivors of the Great War* (Leo Cooper, 1998).
Lyn Macdonald, *1914–1918: Voices and Images of the Great War Imagined* (Michael Joseph, 1988).
Jon Lewis, *True World War 1 Stories* (Robinson, 1997).

6 Primary Sources

All these memoirs, novels, diaries, letters and poems were written by people with experience of the war. Students may also consult unpublished primary source material at the Imperial War Museum.
Richard Aldington, *Death of a Hero* (World Distributors, 1965).
Henri Barbusse, *Under Fire* (Everyman's Library, 1969).
Alan Bishop & Mark Bostridge (eds), *Letters from a Lost Generation* (Abacus, 1998).
Robert Blake (ed), *Private Papers of Douglas Haig* (Eyre & Spottiswoode, 1952).
Vera Brittain, *Testament of Youth* (Victor Gollancz, 1933).
Winston Churchill, *The World Crisis: 1911–1918* (Odham's Press, 1938).
John Dos Passos, *Three Soldiers* (Penguin, 1990).
Florence Farmborough, *A Nurse at the Russian Front* (Constable, 1974).
Brian Gardner, *Up the Line to Death: The War Poets* (Methuen, 1964).
Jon Glover & Jon Silkin, *The Penguin Book of First World War Prose* (Penguin, 1989).
Robert Graves, *Goodbye To All That* (Penguin, 1960).
Ernest Hemingway, *A Farewell To Arms* (Arrow, 1994).
David Lloyd George, *War Memoirs* (Odham's Press, 1938).
Frederic Manning, *Her Privates We* (Serpent's Tail, 1999)
Eric Maria Remarque, *All Quiet on the Western Front* (Putnam's, 1929).
Siegfried Sassoon, *Diaries 1915–1918* (Faber & Faber, 1983).
Siegfried Sassoon, *The Complete Memoirs of George Sherston* (Faber & Faber, 1972).
Trudi Tate (ed.), *Women, Men and the Great War: An anthology of stories* (Manchester University Press).
Edwin Vaughan, *Some Desperate Glory* (Macmillan, 1987).
Henry Williamson, *How Dear Is Life* (Alan Sutton, 1995).

Index